IMPACTFUL INCLUSIVE LEADERSHIP

9 POWERFUL STRATEGIES THAT ENCOURAGE DIVERSITY, FOSTER EQUITY, AND CULTIVATE INCLUSIVITY TO TRANSFORM YOUR WORKPLACE

MARGUERITE ALLOLDING

SHE LEADS
STRATEGIES LLC

1st Editon

Author: Marguerite Allolding

Publisher: She Leads Strategies, LLC

CONTENTS

CONTENT WARNING

Chapter 9 includes discussions about workplace discrimination and bias, which may evoke strong emotional responses or memories for some individuals. Please proceed with empathy and self-care. If you feel triggered or overwhelmed, consider taking a break or seeking support.

INTRODUCTION

~

In the heart of bustling workplaces today, the promise of diversity, equity, and inclusion (DEI) echoes, and more placards and persistent voices are speaking about it. However, a tale still needs to be explored as many keep silent on the sensitive part of DEI. Imagine Sarah, a talented Gen Z professional, bursting with innovative ideas and hungrily navigating the corporate labyrinth. Despite her brilliance, she encounters subtle barriers, a stark reminder that generational divides persist. This scenario isn't isolated; it reflects a broader narrative where the vibrant energy of youth is met with systemic challenges.

Racial discrimination also stubbornly lingers, acting as a setback for many in the professional arena. The pursuit of workplace equality proves elusive for individuals with disabilities, while women continue to face the subtle yet pervasive currents of gender bias. Amidst this landscape, people of color confront pronounced prejudices, and those embracing diverse genders and orientations find themselves subjected to unfair treatment. In the collective pursuit of

DEI, it becomes evident that despite progress, significant struggles linger in our quest for a truly inclusive working environment. Let's delve into the nuanced realities that shape our professional landscape, exploring the challenges that demand our attention and collective action.

Perhaps you've found yourself in that zone? You're in this workspace, feeling undervalued and overlooked for promotions, facing unfair treatment, and now experiencing discrimination has become your narrative. It's a subtle yet impactful undertone that makes you question your worth, your contributions seemingly eclipsed. So, because you are witnessing stereotypical behaviors and discriminatory practices, it stirs a sense of awakening to the diversity of the world around you and how this workplace keeps you from the bigger picture. You're acutely aware of your potential and eager to contribute more. Yet, the acknowledgment you seek remains elusive, and the promises of change seem slim when familiar faces continue to ascend the corporate ladder. Despite your studies, experience, and hard work, the payoff and hopes to become a senior executive are disproportionate, leaving you grappling with the frustration of unfulfilled assurances of "you're next in line" or "better luck next year." So, who have you become because of this? A breeding ground of discontent fueled by a lack of passion for the job, knowing DEI is nothing more than an abbreviation with no actualization. Hating where you work becomes a rational response when efforts are met with unequal rewards, so you ponder the unsettling question: "Why does the same effort yield disparate outcomes?"

Simple! The answer lies in front of you. It's you!

You are the reason things remain the same: you fail to make your dissatisfaction known so every other workplace can take DEI as a personal concern. The pains you experience can only be the beginning of an idea to turn the system around through an awakening of how inequality and non-inclusion are not condoned and accepted as business as usual. While HR and high-level executives typically wield the power to enact decisions and reforms, the persistent cycle of unfair treatment has left you weary and disheartened. Your sincere desire for a workplace defined by DEI stems from the belief that everyone should reap the rewards of their hard work. Empowered by this conviction, you stand poised to instigate change, whether you witness a deficit of inclusion or personally experience its effects. Hence, the need for this book to come into play for you:

- Reading this book will expose you to diverse viewpoints, so you have an above-the-surface understanding of the intricacies of DEI coming from your perspective and that of other different groups.
- There is no doubt about the level of insight to be gained from this literary work, as it will empower you to make informed decisions to the point where you are equipped with the knowledge to advocate for and implement meaningful changes in your workplace. Once you understand that you are the change you seek, you become driven toward actualizing it.
- A well-versed understanding of DEI principles gained through reading is a powerful catalyst, motivating and enabling you to actively contribute to being the lightbulb fostering a more inclusive and equitable work environment.

These are only but a few of the numerous benefits this book will provide you. It's a whole new journey into taking ownership of your rightful position in the workplace, so no one makes you believe you're there by luck instead of a well-deserved role. Did I mention the ton of results moving forward? Here are just FIVE:

1. **Updated Leadership:** You will gain a comprehensive understanding of how embracing diversity and ensuring equity can elevate your leadership, resulting in workplaces that thrive on the richness of varied perspectives.

2. **Effective Advocacy:** Empowered with insights from the book, you will have the confidence to champion fairness and inclusivity actively. You are the influential voices for positive workplace transformations that transcend biases and discrimination.

3. **Enhanced Team Dynamics:** With team members, you can foster environments where collaboration is more than just a buzzword—it will be a reality that propels teams toward unparalleled success.

4. **Improved Organizational Culture:** As a cultural architect, you will play a pivotal role in shaping workplaces that prioritize respect so the atmosphere is where everyone feels a sense of belonging and shared purpose.

5. **Professional Growth:** Beyond skill development, understanding and embracing diversity pushes you toward a path of continuous self-improvement, establishing them as change agents capable of driving progress within your professional spheres.

Why am I the best person to tell you this?

I have lived and breathed the corporate world for a number of years. I emerged as a pioneering figure with a rich leadership background spanning more than two decades in the professional field. Settling in New Jersey at the age of 44, I built a life alongside my devoted husband and two delightful children. However, my narrative came to life in a quaint town and unfolded further in the corporate landscape of Chicago before reaching the bustling metropolis of New York. Along this trajectory, I occupied numerous prestigious leadership positions within both expansive corporations and more intimate organizational settings, consistently shattering barriers and redefining expectations.

Honestly, it wasn't easy at the time, but many things became clear to me. I personally witnessed the immense, yet neglected, potential residing in numerous talented women and smaller demographics, often dismissed and undervalued. This ignited a profound passion within me to empower women, amplify their voices, and serve as the inspiration behind my first book, *Fearless Female Leadership*.

I delved into testing methods and strategies suitable for contemporary settings, incorporating data-driven analysis and leveraging DEI principles. Through rigorous research, I uncovered distinctive steps that proved beneficial for a diverse spectrum of individuals, extending beyond the realm of women alone.

It brought me where I am today. A woman who is passionate about making every human being feel relevant within the next place they call home: the workspace. If you have this desire as I do, then you've come to the right place. You can embark on this life-changing journey by embracing the initial move and as you gear up to infuse data-driven DEI principles into your workplace. Get ready to nurture a vibrant, diverse, and wholly inclusive environment.

1

WORKPLACE DEI 101
UNDERSTAND THE ENEMY BEFORE CHANGING IT

Strength lies in differences, not in similarities.
—Covey S. (1989)

#1—Unveiling the DEI Revolution: The Might of Awareness

Were you aware that in today's ever-evolving corporate landscape, an astonishing 75% of organizations accord the highest precedence to DEI (Diversity, Equity, and Inclusion), considering it an indispensable keystone for their future prosperity? These statistics are beyond a trend, but an imperative for advancement and development, which is why, in this chapter, you will be taken on a journey into the core of DEI so that, armed with knowledge and profound insights, you will be endowed with the capability to reshape work environments, cultivate inclusivity, and institute lasting transformation.

#2—DEI: When Did It Become So Relevant?

If this term comes to you as just another abbreviation introduced among the long list of shorter terms for reinventing how humanity can be more encompassing, think again. DEI is more than a term. It's a movement seeking to ensure every workplace environment creates comfortable and embracing room for all kinds of people irrespective of nationality, religion, gender, abilities, or sexual orientation.

DEI is a framework that organizations use consistently because, although they mean different things, they are interconnected in transforming the workplace. Let's see what they encompass:

- **Diversity** is having individuals with various backgrounds, experiences, and characteristics within an organization or community. It doesn't matter what race, gender, ethnicity, age, sexual orientation, physical abilities, religion, or socioeconomic status these people represent. Their diverse identities and perspectives make them exceptional in the environment they embrace.
- **Equity** ensures everyone has the same opportunities, resources, and advantages within an organization or society. It involves recognizing and addressing systemic barriers and biases that may hinder certain groups from achieving their full potential. In essence, equity seeks that leveled playing field so everyone has a fair chance at success. It's what John Legend, the famous musician and activist, stated when asked about his thoughts on DEI.
- **Inclusion**, however, is a practice of fostering a culture of value, respect, and empowerment for people to contribute their unique perspectives and talents. It goes beyond having a diverse workforce; it's about fully participating, collaborating, and thriving so those diverse voices are heard and no one feels excluded or marginalized.

Verna Myers, a prominent advocate for diversity and inclusion, defines it all in more relatable terms this way: "Diversity is 'being invited to the party' (representation), equity is 'being asked to dance' (fair treatment), and inclusion is 'dancing like nobody's watching' (feeling valued and empowered)" (Myers, 2022).

#3—DEI Interconnects Differently

It shows that these three elements are different principles interwoven to provide a holistic approach toward workplace success and productivity. So, what does each element represent?

- Diversity is the "**what**" about various people and perspectives.
- Equity is the "**how**" of the actions and policies that ensure fair hearing and justice, thereby removing barriers.
- Inclusion is the "**how well**" measure of how effectively an organization embraces and values diversity, creating an inclusive culture.

For example, if individuals from diverse backgrounds do not feel welcomed and empowered (inclusion), we need more than diversity initiatives, we need efforts to address systematic biases (equity). However, these equity measures may not lead to meaningful change if the workplace culture does not embrace diversity and actively include underrepresented groups. In the entertainment industry, which has been one of the most active grounds aiming to uphold DEI, the iconic actor Denzel Washington emphasized that for him, DEI from the angle of equity is: "Opening doors for people who have been historically underrepresented and ensuring they have a chance to succeed" (Commencement Speech, University of Pennsylvania, May 2011).

This is not only true but a requirement to lead to Inclusion as that bridge that ties diversity and equity together, ensuring that the benefits of a diverse workforce are fully realized.

#4—The Different Sides to Each Element

One of the strengths of DEI is that it considers various aspects of each element, thereby introducing a range of perspectives that enhance workplace effectiveness. When it comes to "diversity", there can be:

- **Demographic Diversity:** In this setting, you find differences related to observable characteristics such as race, ethnicity, gender, age, sexual orientation, disability, religion, and nationality. Here, creativity and teamwork thrive as each individual brings their idea of problem-solving to the table.
- **Cognitive Diversity:** The thoughts and intellectual approaches to issues are diverse and intuitive, bringing innovative solutions from multiple angles.
- **Experiential Diversity:** Your life experience and background are as important to shaping a workplace as another. Once you bring it to the forefront, it creates room for a better understanding of individual opinions on every issue. No judgments are made; rather, the fact that you have an experience to share makes the environment more relaxing for everyone to work together harmoniously.
- **Generational Diversity:** It's beautiful to see the Baby Boomers, Generation X, Millennials, and Generation Z all in a workplace because of the power of DEI, as each comes in with a unique work style that each generation can learn from.

In "equity", you find:

- **Procedural Equity:** Ensuring that the processes and procedures within an organization or system are fair and unbiased, from hiring practices to decision-making processes. The goal is for all applicants to feel confident in the system, knowing their qualifications matter more than their background and orientation.

- **Outcome Equity:** Focusing on fair outcomes or results, regardless of initial disparities. In a classroom, students of all backgrounds have access to quality education, and the graduation rates rise, bridging the achievement gap so fairness is upheld.
- **Structural Equity:** Addressing systemic and structural inequalities perpetuating discrimination and inequity, like unequal pay due to gender inequality, is the norm. No woman should feel her gender in the workplace will place her on a lower cadre for promotion or higher pay. Rather, the policies must ensure gender equality to the latter.
- **Economic Equity:** Ensuring that individuals have equal access to economic opportunities and resources. Every community should invest in job training programs to help marginalized groups access opportunities for financial stability and reduce wealth and income disparities where the rich get richer and the poor get poorer. This is the origin of capitalist societies, where class and status are put above creating a comfortable standard of living for all to enjoy.
- **Educational Equity:** All students should have equal access to quality education, regardless of their background. In societies where education seems underfunded, all it takes is a leveled playground to create educational opportunities for all, and the learning must always feel more encompassing. The disparity between public and private schools should not determine the curriculum system and the post-graduation opportunities the students will encounter in the workplace environment. As long as you are good, you deserve to be given a fair chance to exhibit your skills anywhere.

Now, like a tree with diversity and equity as the branches, what stem cells help make "inclusion" the connecting ground for sustainability?

Cultural Inclusion: Inclusion is mostly about value creation, so when you have people from several cultural backgrounds come together, it opens the door to celebrating cultural traditions and fostering cross-cultural understanding. Imagine a workplace where people are encouraged to come for events that showcase cultural displays in food, music, and more. It won't only be a successful way of driving home the essence of inclusion, but it will be the beginning of building long-term ties of cultural appreciation.

- **Professional Inclusion:** For employees to desire to be part of any workplace environment, one of the key attractions is having equal access to career development, advancement opportunities, and mentorship, regardless of their identity. No individual wants to feel bored or redundant in a system that doesn't encourage career growth because, in such places, the chances for promotion and recognition would be slim, and the hope for a pay raise would be a pipe dream. There must always be a consistent working plan for job satisfaction, leading to organizational productivity.
- **Social Inclusion:** A workplace doesn't need to feel uptight just because it's a work environment. The room to socialize and connect should be a welcome way to build positive relationships, networks, and a sense of belonging. If you belong to the working class, you would understand that the next home after the home is the workplace, and it's why having a supportive community of bosses and colleagues makes the workplace feel like a home away from home.
- **Psychological Safety:** If you're in an environment where you have to look around you before you speak up and share your ideas, then there is a problem. Inclusion encourages respect for opinions, so you must always feel comfortable taking risks and stating your case even if it hurts. It's how people learn, grow, unlearn, and relearn for better system structure.
- **Intersectional Inclusion:** It is crucial to recognize that individuals have multiple aspects of their identity and

ensure their unique needs and experiences are considered and respected. For instance, medical staff should consider patients' cultural backgrounds and health conditions within a healthcare setting. This dual consideration facilitates the provision of care that is not only more effective but also empathetic.

Intersectionality

Understanding the concept of intersectionality goes beyond looking at one aspect of your identity in isolation. It's not just about your gender or race but the multiple dimensions of identity and social categories and how they intersect and interact with one another to establish the histories surrounding discrimination and privilege. Kimberlé Crenshaw, a legal scholar and civil rights advocate, coined it. For her, intersectionality could be likened to a situation in which a Black woman may face distinct discrimination from that experienced by a White woman or a Black man due to the combined effects of racism and sexism. A situation that is detrimental not only to the workplace or the working class but to an entire world system and the reason why Martin Luther King Jr. would say, *"Injustice anywhere is a threat to Justice everywhere"* (King 1963). With this statement, it is clear that intersectionality aims to encourage a more nuanced and comprehensive understanding of social inequalities and emphasizes the need to address various aspects of identity simultaneously when addressing issues related to diversity, equity, and inclusion.

In this regard, certain policies have been introduced in line with intersectionality to assist in weighing the parameters of organizational success between business goals, job satisfaction, and delivery.

DIVERSITY
- Demographic Diversity
- Cognitive Diversity
- Experiential Diversity
- Generational Diversity

INCLUSION
- Cultural Inclusion
- Professional Inclusion
- Social Inclusion:
- Psychological Safety
- Intersectional Inclusion

EQUITY
- Procedural Equity
- Outcome Equity
- Structural Equity
- Economic Equity
- Educational Equity

ESG (Environmental, Social, and Governance)

Policies that represent a framework companies and investors use to evaluate a company's impact on society and the environment beyond its financial performance. Each component of ESG represents a different aspect:

- **Environmental (E):** What is a company's environmental impact? Here, factors such as carbon emissions, energy efficiency, waste management, and sustainability practices are considered and evaluated.
- **Social (S):** A company's relationships with its employees, customers, suppliers, and communities where labor practices, employee well-being, and community engagement stand as a strong ground for assessing the success of an organization.

- **Governance (G):** It refers to how a company is managed and the structures in place to ensure ethical and responsible decision-making. It includes issues such as board diversity, executive compensation, and transparency in financial reporting.

ESG policies are used to assess a company's broader societal and environmental responsibilities. They are increasingly important for investors and consumers who want to support businesses that align with their values and prioritize sustainability. It's important that these policies are never ignored or taken for granted if a brand is to stand.

CSR (Corporate Social Responsibility Policies)

It's a company's voluntary effort to contribute positively to society and the environment. CSR initiatives go beyond legal and regulatory requirements and often involve philanthropy, ethical business practices, and efforts to mitigate a company's negative impacts. Call them the charity bodies that see society as a place that consistently needs support in every way. Their initiative can include:

- Charitable donations to community organizations.
- Environmental sustainability efforts, such as reducing carbon emissions or conserving natural resources.
- Ethical sourcing and supply chain practices like good inventory management, having resourceful forecasting to project the demand and supply of products, or even risk management that can handle the mitigation of environmental disasters to sustainable development.
- Employee volunteer programs and efforts to promote workplace diversity and inclusion.
- Transparency in business operations and ethical marketing.

It can go on and on, but what's certain is that CSR is about a company's commitment to being a responsible corporate citizen by actively addressing social and environmental issues.

Ultimately, DEI incorporates some ESG and CSR policies and frameworks to ensure intersectionality and diverse inclusion are priorities within a company's policies. You want to instill a sense of belonging and responsibility in your workplace.

Looking at it statistically, McKinsey & Company affirms that diversity and equity matter today because Companies with diverse executive teams are 25–36% more likely to have above-average profitability. Also, an inclusive-minded workplace outperforms less inclusive ones because diverse leadership is 33% more likely to have industry-leading profitability (McKinsey & Company, 2020).

#5—Benefits of DEI

The Bulletin, on their part, states that equity ensures a fair shot at success, breaking down systemic barriers. The statistical data and confirmations above show that the BENEFITS of DEI in the workplace are limitless. To be more specific, DEI ensures:

- **Healthier Working Space:** Prioritizing DEI creates a healthier, more inclusive workplace culture. Fostering a sense of belonging, respect, and fairness among employees ultimately leading to higher morale, reduced stress, and improved mental well-being.
- **Top Talent Attraction and Retention:** Companies that value DEI are more appealing to a diverse pool of candidates seeking career advancement. Moreover, an inclusive workplace is more likely to retain employees who know their onions and are irreplaceable in terms of turnover costs and encouraging a stable and committed workforce.
- **Topnotch Decision-Making and Innovation:** Diverse perspectives and experiences are always the main menu,

leading to better decision-making and innovative solutions to challenges. When you have a workplace heavy with diverse thoughts due to cultural differences and experiences, it can give organizations a competitive edge in a rapidly changing business landscape.

- **High Profitability and Brand Reputation:** The DEI strategies often begets increased profitability, as diverse leadership and inclusive practices correlate with higher financial performance, an enhanced brand reputation, and a dedication to social issues.

- **Legal Compliance and Ethical Responsibility:** Undoubtedly, organizations dedicated to making DEI their motto for success always seek to comply with anti-discrimination laws and regulations. They channel their ethical responsibility to create a fair and just workplace that values all individuals, irrespective of their background identity or encircled personality.

Challenges for Workplaces Lacking DEI Initiatives

To understand this perspective clearly, you must access data that unveils the stark realities within workplaces lacking Diversity, Equity, and Inclusion (DEI) initiatives. These statistics shed light on the common challenges individuals encounter in such environments, and you may have a story that connects you to these data samples. As we delve deeper into DEI strategies, you'll find more data samples and perhaps bring about scenarios you have observed in your workplace.

- **Bias in Hiring:** Over the years, it has been shown in many ways that individuals with African American names can experience bias in hiring, potentially hindering interview opportunities and bringing workplace discrimination. This affects 25% of African Americans, Latinx, and Hispanics, impacting job satisfaction and well-being. Consider two equally qualified job applicants: Jamal Jackson and John Smith. Jamal, with a distinctly African-American name, might face subtle biases during initial screening, potentially resulting in John being selected for an interview despite their similar qualifications. This illustrates how implicit biases can impact interview opportunities. Or, imagine Maria, a Latina employee, who, despite her qualifications, is passed over for opportunities, and her contributions often go unrecognized. This discrimination affects her job satisfaction and overall well-being, highlighting the issue of workplace bias and its negative consequences.

- **Racial Workforce Disparity:** It's not new to discover that 77%, of the workforce in the United States remains Caucasian, highlighting the need for diversity efforts (De Jager, 2023). It's what Viola Davis, an acclaimed actress known for her roles in films and television, had been outspoken about when advocating for diversity and inclusion in the entertainment industry. She has openly discussed the disparities faced by actors of color, particularly African Americans, regarding limited opportunities, unequal pay, and underrepresentation in leading roles.
- **Disparity in Promotions:** Gender disparities persist in promotions, with fewer women reaching managerial positions, and when you know about women like Oprah Winfey in the media industry, it resonates with the journey of most women who fight to secure their positions in every organization to date.
- **Gender Pay Gap:** The gender pay gap persists, and the likes of tennis legend Serena Williams was a victim as she became vocal about the gender pay gap in professional tennis. Despite her incredible success and achievements, she has pointed out disparities in prize money between male and female tennis players, highlighting the need for pay equity in sports. Why should women receive lower salary increases despite seeking equal pay raises? They put in just as much as

the males, and the sport isn't made easy just because it's a woman playing, so there should be no limitations.

- **Barriers for Disabled and LGBTQ+ Individuals:** People with disabilities face limited job opportunities, while LGBTQ+ and gender-diverse individuals encounter discrimination affecting their job satisfaction and health. Marlee Matlin, the acclaimed deaf actress, shared her experiences of being typecast in roles specifically for deaf characters rather than having equal chances to play a wide range of roles. Her advocacy today has called attention to the need for greater inclusivity and open doors for disabled actors. It doesn't end there; LGBTQ+ individuals have had their fair share of workplace discrimination. In 2019, a U.S. Supreme Court case (Bostock v. Clayton County) highlighted workplace discrimination against LGBTQ+ employees. The case involved Gerald Bostock, who was fired from his job after his employer discovered he was gay. The Supreme Court's ruling in favor of Bostock affirmed that LGBTQ+ individuals are protected from workplace discrimination under Title VII of the Civil Rights Act of 1964. Many LGBTQ+ employees have shared experiences of discrimination, microaggressions, and exclusion in the workplace. These scenarios often involve employees being treated differently or unfairly due to their sexual orientation or gender identity. Advocacy and policy changes aim to create more connecting workplaces for LGBTQ+ individuals and the disabled community to ensure no one is left behind in building a more inclusivity-embracing workspace for all.

Also, in 2019, John Legend and other activists launched the "FREE AMERICA" campaign to raise awareness about mass incarceration and advocate for criminal justice reform. The campaign highlighted the stark disparities in sentencing and treating individuals in the criminal justice system. John Legend's involvement and advocacy efforts have contributed to significant changes in criminal justice policies in some U.S. states, bringing attention to the need for fairness and equity within the system.

As we reflect on the benefits of diversity, equity, and inclusion, the undeniable power of data reinforces the urgency for change. If you find yourself among the statistics that reveal disparities, remember that data doesn't lie. It serves as a compass guiding us toward strategies for meaningful transformation. If you're ready to foster diversity, equity, and inclusion in your workplace, let's move forward to the next chapter. Strategy two will help you delve deeper into analyzing the need, a crucial step before you can pave the way for effective and lasting changes.

2

ANALYZING THE NEED FOR DEI IN THE WORKPLACE

Decisions are rarely black and white. By analyzing and collaborating effectively, we can uncover better solutions.
—Jamie Dimon (BrainyQuote, 2001)

The Key to Identifying a Non-DEI-Oriented Workplace

Have you ever encountered the term "having a nuanced understanding of a challenge?" Well, it's not just about staring the problem in the face and thinking up a solution based on mind and sight assessment; it's crucially strategic for initiating change. This assessment involves in-depth examination, including surveys, focus groups, and interviews, to identify specific issues faced by underrepresented groups where DEI is concerned. This is called the Lighthouse Framework, a strategic blueprint for identifying and addressing DEI challenges and opportunities within an organization. The framework consists of several key components:

- **Data Collection and Analysis:** This first step involves surveys, interviews, focus groups, and other methods. This data is then meticulously analyzed to gain a deep understanding of the current state of DEI within the organization.

- **Comprehensive Assessment:** Organizations comprehensively assess their workplace environment, policies, and practices. This assessment includes examining employees' experiences from diverse demographic groups, identifying barriers to inclusion, and recognizing opportunities for improvement.
- **Pinpoint Specific Issues:** The framework emphasizes pinpointing specific DEI challenges underrepresented groups face. This includes recognizing areas where disparities exist and understanding the root causes of these disparities.
- **Create Targeted Strategies:** Armed with a nuanced understanding of DEI challenges, organizations can develop targeted strategies and initiatives to address the identified issues and create a more inclusive workplace.
- **Continuous Improvement:** The DEI Lighthouse Framework promotes a commitment to ongoing improvement. Organizations are encouraged to regularly review and assess their DEI efforts, making necessary adjustments and refinements to ensure progress.
- **Inclusive Leadership:** Leadership plays a crucial role in the framework, emphasizing inclusive leadership practices. Leaders are expected to champion DEI initiatives, set the tone for the organization, and lead by example.
- **Transparency and Accountability:** Organizations here must embrace communication as their DEI goals, progress openly, and hold themselves accountable for achieving meaningful results.
- **Employee Engagement:** Engaging employees from diverse backgrounds is a central component. By actively seeking input and feedback from employees, they get involved in decision-making, creating a sense of belonging.

- **Measurable Metrics:** The framework emphasizes the importance of using measurable metrics to track progress. One must define key performance indicators (KPIs) related to DEI and regularly assess their performance against these metrics.
- **Cultural Shift:** Ultimately, the DEI Lighthouse Framework aims to foster a cultural shift within the organization. It seeks to embed DEI principles into the organization's DNA, creating a workplace where diversity is celebrated, equity is prioritized, and inclusion is the norm.

In doing this, there will surely be a holistic approach to enhancing diversity, equity, and inclusion through policies, practices, and cultural aspects. That said, workplaces will set their priorities right in identifying the roadmap to success. For most, two things stand out:

1. **Gender Equity:** In gender equity, organizations recognize the importance of addressing gender disparities and inequalities in the workplace. The red flags are raised, especially in times of promotion and pay rates, which calls for the DEI initiative to set the pace for what is needed to achieve equilibrium among colleagues regardless of identity or biological formation.
2. **Competitive Standing:** With the DEI initiatives, competitive standing is imperative to help organizations foster diversity and inclusion for improved performance and competitiveness. Once a place is open to change, the opportunities for growth and productivity are endless.

To effectively prioritize successful roadmap initiatives, it is crucial to evaluate DEI not merely as a broadly accepted necessity but also as a distinct, individualized reality. This approach involves thoroughly examining the intricacies of non-DEI existence, identifying its roots, and actively minimizing its presence.

Evaluation and Assessment

Organizations can begin the mission of finding the loopholes using several personal methods of evaluation and assessment of non-DEI existence in the workplace:

- **Self-Assessment Surveys:** Employees can participate in self-assessment surveys that gauge their feelings of inclusion, opportunities for growth, and perceptions of bias or discrimination. These surveys often include questions about workplace culture, interactions with colleagues, and career advancement.

An example is Anabelle, a long-term employee with a construction company, who participated in a self-assessment survey asking about her sense of belonging. She shared, "The survey made me reflect on my experiences, and I realized I hadn't felt truly included. It led to conversations with HR, and they've since initiated changes to create a more inclusive environment."

- **Feedback and Reporting:** Implement a confidential feedback and reporting mechanism where employees can report bias, discrimination, or exclusion incidents. This allows individuals to share their experiences and helps organizations address issues in real time. Mark, an employee from Chicago who had just been recruited as a customer support for a bank and was in training, stated that:

When I had a concern about a microaggression while starting off and shadowing a senior manager, I used our reporting mechanism to share my ordeal of feeling uncomfortable with the show of harshness in getting the job done. I appreciated the confidentiality as it made me feel free to express my concerns without reservation. In fact, it led to a conversation with my manager, and the issue was addressed promptly, showing that the organization takes DEI seriously.

- **Focus Groups and Interviews:** During a focus group discussion, Maria shared her experience, saying she felt heard when she spoke about how being a person with a disability made her afraid of how the workspace would embrace her. She attested that there was no blame, but about making things better, as she was reminded, she is just as relevant as the next person who doesn't have a disability. For her, it meant she could be optimistic about DEI because the efforts made to create a sense of value and respect were established.

When organizations conduct focus group discussions or interviews with employees to delve deeper into their experiences and gather qualitative insights, these interactions allow employees to express their concerns and speak openly about what changes can make a difference.

- **Individual Goals:** Did you know that evaluating an individual's career progression, opportunities, and achievements within the organization can reveal potential biases? In doing so, questions such as: Are promotions, raises, and assignments distributed equitably will be brought up? It will draw attention to how this can be fixed for long-term goals.

Alex boldly stated these facts to his supervisor in a training session. He said he noticed a pattern in promotions favoring a particular group of persons, and this was odd for him, who had a long-term record with the organization. Why wasn't he due for a raise or promotion? So, he decided to track his achievements and raise the issue with his manager. So far, so good; he confirmed it worked out for the best as more equitable career opportunities were shifted his way since then. It's about being attentive to your rights as a workplace employee. Never see yourself as unworthy when you know the time and effort you put into the job.

- Mentorship: When you participate in mentorship and sponsorship programs, you will have a clear idea of assessing and accessing career development support. You will also understand that when you do not reap the benefits of mentorships, inclusive group programs, and all kinds of networking, the disparity plays out, and of course, DEI would mean no more than words with no action for you.

Step-by-Step Approach to Assess Work Environment

To make these methods above count, there needs to be a systematic step-by-step approach for leaders to assess their current work environment to ensure that DEI never dwindles or loses its presence but implements a strategy for change.

Step 1: Check the Website—This is usually the quickest way to discover the status of DEI in workplaces. Visit the company's official website and navigate to sections like "About Us," "Our Values," "Mission and Vision," or "Diversity and Inclusion." Look for any written mission statements or commitment to DEI and assess if the tone truly carries the goal of DEI beyond words. Companies often use their websites to communicate their dedication to DEI, and it can be through words, images, and the like so that everyone feels at home when they come into that online space. Take a look at Google. See how they made prominent features of their diversity initiatives for their workplace. It showcased their commitment to creating and sustaining inclusion and made more people realize that Google Group has amazing DEI ethics that go beyond time and personality.

Step 2: Online Data Search—Utilize search engines to find publicly available data and reports related to the company's DEI initiatives. This could include diversity reports, sustainability reports, or articles discussing the organization's diversity and inclusion efforts. Pay attention to any progress or challenges mentioned or, possibly, legal cases where the organization sustained protecting their employee in a situation surrounding discrimination or microaggression. These sorts of reports attract potential employees to desire to work in a space where their interests are utmost. Online platforms like LinkedIn are great spaces to explore the profiles of any company's leaders and employees and their professional backgrounds and affiliations, which mostly reveal insights into diversity efforts.

Step 3: Review Social Media—Scan for posts, articles, or comments related to DEI on social media profiles on platforms like LinkedIn, Twitter, or Facebook. Companies want growth and publicity for the right reasons, and that can best be achieved when they share updates, events, and initiatives related to diversity and inclusion on their social media channels. If there are real-time engagement posts between employees and others who have a passion for DEI, it can make a world of difference in any company's working environment evaluation.

Step 4: Calculate Diversity as it Stands—Gather data on the representation of different demographic groups within the company. This may include statistics on gender, race, ethnicity, age, and more. Look for diversity reports or data available in the company's annual reports or on its website, where you can combine all quantitative data with qualitative findings. Microsoft's diversity dashboard is a good example; it provides real-time data on workforce diversity, promoting transparency and accountability.

Step 5: Check Ratio of Diverse Leaders, Managers, and Team Leaders Existence—The composition of the company's leadership team, including executives, managers, and team leaders, is imperative in assessing whether individuals from diverse backgrounds are well-represented in leadership roles. Apple's CEO, Tim Cook, was, among many things, very passionate and vocal in his advocacy for DEI and its positive impact on the company's culture. For him, it was more like a channel to define how civilization aims to tilt in the direction of harmony if well embraced, as described by the Late Mahatma Gandhi, India's renowned leader.

Step 6: Employee Retention and Satisfaction—Analyze employee retention rates, particularly among diverse employees. How many have worked several years of service and have risen through the ranks? Review employee satisfaction surveys or feedback to identify whether certain demographic groups express lower satisfaction or face higher turnover rates. Are there more Asians speaking out on non-DEI than others? Are the disabled colleagues making cases for issues of inclusion and potential termination threats? These can raise many concerns about where the organization stands in the career growth of diverse employees. You can even conduct informational interviews with employees who represent different demographics. Their personal stories can provide invaluable insights into workplace dynamics.

Step 7: Mentorship or Training Programs—Investigate whether the organization offers mentorship programs or training initiatives focusing on DEI. These programs may include mentoring circles or leadership development opportunities for underrepresented groups. It is transformational and opens the door for all individuals seeking to be mentors and mentees to foster a culture of learning and growth. See how Facebook's Lean In Circles, which was inspired by Sheryl Sandberg's book, encourages mentorship and support among female employees, making them more aware of their gender role in the workplace.

Step 8: Do You Have DEI Training?—Check if the company provides DEI training programs for all employees. This measure helps raise awareness about diversity-related issues, reduce unconscious biases, and promote inclusive behaviors in the workplace. If it's missing, it's a problem. How will employees share meaningful conversations about these issues if they don't dialogue over it? Not every DEI conversation is fashioned to challenge the odds; instead, it becomes the gateway to harnessing positive change for an organization's present and future cultural structure.

Step 9: Check the Incident Reports—Issues relating to discrimination, harassment, or bias within the workplace must not only be reported but examined. Analyzing the frequency and nature of reported incidents and repeated negative trends in a transparent and anonymous fashion creates a room for openness and willingness to express opinions and inhibitions at all times.

Step 10: Do You Have ERG Software?—If the organization has Employee Resource Groups (ERGs) or affinity groups, assess the feedback and engagement levels within these groups. ERGs, which are the employees' voices, often provide valuable insights into their experiences, needs, and areas for improvement. J.H. Douglas (1959) stated, "Our ability to listen and take action on feedback is the secret to excellence." Airbnb is just one of the examples that showcase the vital role ERGs play in providing feedback and shaping the company's policies, including combating discrimination in their bookings. The success story of this brand speaks for itself, as it is now a globally welcoming approach to tourism in comfort.

Step 11: Observe Patterns in Discriminatory Onboarding or Missed Achievements—Investigate patterns of discrimination in various aspects, including the onboarding process, leadership appointments, and missed career advancement opportunities for diverse employees. Identifying these patterns helps pinpoint specific areas for intervention and necessary advocacy for unbiased processes and equal opportunities for all.

Step 12: Consider the Talent Attraction Strategies—Evaluate strategies such as recruitment efforts targeted at diverse communities, partnerships with diversity-focused organizations, or participation in job fairs and events aimed at diverse candidates. Are they compelling enough? Do they proactively show outreach efforts toward talent acquisition? Only time will tell how far and effective the DEI approach has been sustained with all the events put in place.

For you to understand the importance of these steps, imagine your company as a ship sailing through uncharted waters. You need a reliable compass to know if you're on course or if there are stormy seas ahead. These steps are like that compass, helping you gauge your company's current position and shed light on issues such as incident reports, employee grievances, a sense of discontent, and recurring missed opportunities for certain colleagues. With all that valuable information neatly organized in a spreadsheet. It becomes a treasure map with markers at key milestones, helping you measure your progress in fostering DEI.

Remember, DEI is not a one-time voyage; it's a continuous journey. So, you must regularly check your compass, adjusting your course as needed to navigate toward a more inclusive and equitable workplace.

ERG and ENG Software

Recall that in step 10, there was a mention of an ERG software to help checkmate all outcomes from engagements within employees and see the possible recurrency or non-recurrency on issues of DEI as well as the personalities involved. With this assessment mode, you'll find that there is much more to ERGs and its sister software ENGs (Employee Network Groups) in the journey to gathering data and concluding assessments efficiently. It not only assists in having a close to accurate measurement of the current status of the company's DEI, but it also labels out the needed changes that workers and the working environment should have to be DEI-friendly.

When you leverage ERGs and ENGs, you'll observe that it's a powerful way to gather essential data for your DEI assessment. Instead of the usual emails that might go unresponded or seen, these groups serve as bridges between your organization and its diverse workforce, offering a safe space for employees to share their DEI experiences. You can actually use these groups to conduct tailored surveys, focus groups, and interviews that capture a wide range of perspectives. Consider an ERG software platform where a Women in Tech group hosts a virtual panel discussion on gender diversity in the tech industry. The software allows members to register, participate in the discussion, and provide feedback afterward.

This promotes engagement and collects valuable data on what women in the organization think about gender-related issues in their field.

The ERG software is the key to enhanced engagement and feedback collection, thereby streamlining ERG and ENG management and acting as a central hub for group activities. To make the most of ERG software, it's essential to cultivate an inclusive culture and encourage active employee participation in these groups. Remember, ERG software thrives when employees are motivated and feel supported in sharing their insights and experiences. If your company selects the Affirmity ERG platform with its robust analytics capabilities, the platform will allow the organization to track the impact of its ERGs over time. That's when you will notice a significant increase in engagement and a decrease in diversity-related complaints since implementing the software, which showcases tangible progress in its DEI efforts.

Now, don't get lost; the Affirmity ERG platform is one of several other ways data is being collected. Undoubtedly, the diversity leaders and HR teams are struggling to keep up with the evolution of DEI in the workplace. However, Affirmity's tools are the key to unlocking the full potential of workplace diversity through Employee Resource Groups (ERGs). These tools empower HR and diversity leaders to foster ERGs that drive leadership development, retain and nurture existing diverse talent, boost recruitment efforts, and streamline the onboarding process. Once you have Affirmity's solutions at hand, organizations can create an environment where employees are engaged, valued, and committed, ultimately leading to a more diverse and inclusive workplace that thrives.

Another great tool is the Qooper. Ever heard of it? Well, like Affirmity, it's an innovative tool that aims to enhance the effectiveness of ERG and ENG using some key elements of success:

- Qooper allows ERG leaders to manage their groups efficiently, facilitating communication, event planning, and collaboration among members.
- The platform enables the creation and management of mentorship programs essential for leadership development and knowledge sharing within ERGs.
- Qooper provides a centralized repository for ERGs to share resources, documents, and best practices, ensuring easy access for all members.
- It offers tools for collecting feedback and conducting surveys to gauge the effectiveness of ERG initiatives and gather insights from members.
- With Qooper, you get analytics and reporting features that help ERG leaders measure their impact, track progress, and make data-driven decisions.
- Best of all, the platform is designed to be mobile-friendly, allowing members to participate and engage with their ERGs from anywhere.

There is also Chezie, another champion of the ERG and ENG movement, and although these platforms support the journey to power up the DEI commitment in the workplace, they have their different strengths. Chezie stands out with a strong mentorship and resource-sharing focus, offering feedback tools and analytics. Affirmity specializes in data analytics and provides comprehensive diversity solutions and consulting services. Qooper, on the other hand, is a versatile platform known for scalability and integration with HR systems.

So, the choice depends on an organization's unique needs and priorities for fostering diversity and inclusion. Not to mention, as much as these tools revamp the power of technology in the pursuit of DEI assessment, it doesn't in any way negate the manual manner of data collection. It's still as effective as ever, and with the help of polls and surveys, complex data are retrieved and broken down, leaving no stone unturned in comprehending the challenges and needed changes surrounding the workplace and DEI.

Conducting Surveys

You can choose how you want to do it. What's more, is that statistics and data will always share with you the effectiveness and efficiency of all polls and survey strategies.

Types of Surveys

1. **Employee Engagement Surveys:** They come in various types, such as satisfaction surveys, vision surveys, leadership surveys, enablement surveys, recognition surveys, and more. Each type focuses on different aspects of employee engagement, and as specific as they come, it spells out data according to that particular tentacle of DEI and has a higher percentage of concern to the organization. Microsoft uses employee surveys to measure various factors, including job satisfaction and leadership effectiveness. They have made data-driven changes based on employee feedback, showcasing the importance of regular surveys.

2. **Sample Surveys:** You can use sample surveys from the provided source to create effective surveys for collecting data in your workplace. A human resources manager can find a sample satisfaction survey from the provided source. Then, they customize it for their organization to measure employee job satisfaction and identify improvement areas. These samples can cover various engagement themes regarding career development, leading to a long-term DEI assessment.

3. **Anonymity for Honest Feedback:** To ensure you receive honest and unbiased feedback, it's essential to maintain anonymity during surveys, polls, and quizzes. This helps employees feel comfortable sharing their thoughts and concerns. Research done by O.C. Tanner found that 79% of

employees who quit their jobs cited a lack of appreciation as a key reason for leaving (Tanner, 2023). It means you, as much as the next employee, want to know you aren't seen as a working machine but as someone whose work counts for something important. Casual as it might sound, it's an essential part of welfare.

4. **Digital Surveys with Google Forms:** It's a convenient tool for conducting digital surveys. It's user-friendly and accessible, making it suitable for smaller teams and organizations.

5. **Culture Amp:** Here is an excellent choice for employee engagement surveys. It offers a comprehensive platform that covers the employee experience, from onboarding to exit, which is so encompassing and makes even the exit of any employee feel at home with no drama or tension.

6. **Connecteam for Hybrid or Remote Workers:** It supports surveys and helps manage teams, making it valuable for organizations with hybrid or remote work setups. It facilitates tasks like scheduling and communication, which is why, in the heat of the COVID-19 pandemic, Hybrid work became unavoidable. It was due to over 70% of established survey facts from employees stating the necessity for flexibility and adaptability (OECD, 2021).

Now you see why companies like Facebook's Meta Platform Inc., SalesForce, and LinkedIn all stand out. They pay attention to employment engagement like a mother to her child. According to Mercer, 92% of companies use employee surveys as a tool to assess and improve employee engagement (Mercer, 2023). The Society for Human Resource Management (SHRM) even found that 77% of organizations offering employee wellness programs boost engagement and well-being (Miller, 2019). When the Work Institute suggested that 42 million employees would leave their jobs in 2021, it wasn't just a statement but a survey of how employee turnover remains a challenge for many organizations if DEI is handled with kid gloves (Work

Institute, 2022). Now more than ever, there needs to be a hunger to face the challenges, fix them, and aim for a positive change.

To do this, it's your turn to create a custom spreadsheet. Start with the first column for the current situation, the second for supporting metrics, and the third for potential complications. The fourth column is where you outline your proposed resolutions. Leave the fifth column empty for now; you'll use it to measure success later. In upcoming chapters, we'll fill in columns 3 and 4 based on data insights and tailored solutions specific to your workplace.

Check the sample below for guidance.

THE SITUATIONAL ASSESSMENT CHART

	1	2	3	4	5
	Current Situation	Data Supporting the Current Situation	Possible Complications Resulting From the Current Situation	Potential Resolutions/Ideas to Improve the Current Situation	New Data After 3 Months of Testing the Resolution
1	• Employees don't feel that the hiring process is fair.	• 9/18/23 employees listed the same issue.	• Poor employee retention and a lack of diversity.	• Change the hiring process to include equitable processes based on people's skills, and post new job listings on diverse job boards.	• 12/6/23 Employees believe the hiring process is more fair. • Alternatively, the sample data could show: 12/6 employees now list a new problem showing the lack of in-house promotions. • (This 3-month metric73 reveals a new problem altogether)

EXAMPLE

Always remember that before embarking on the journey to transform your workplace culture and policies, it's essential to understand people's needs. To achieve this, you must gather input from your colleagues and assess the true state of your work environment. You must know that you cannot fix a broken system unless you take the pains to note what really went wrong and how it can be amended.

PITCHING A NEW WORKPLACE CULTURE THAT MATTERS

It's not what you look at that matters; it's what you see.
—H.D. Thoreau (*Gracious Quotes, 2023*)

What Makes a DEI Idea Successful?

The answer is simple: Achieving success with your DEI initiatives and embarking on a transformative journey from start to finish. As H. Ford (1923) aptly said, "Coming together is a beginning; keeping together is progress; working together is a success." Therefore, for the success of your DEI ideas, you must prioritize them within your organizational strategy and recognize their role in shaping a better future.

McKinsey's "Diversity, Equity, and Inclusion Lighthouses 2023" report highlights that creating lasting change begins with delving into best practices and understanding how they can guide your efforts. You set a clear course and ensure your initiatives resonate with your organization's mission. As a ship relies on its compass, your DEI journey hinges on these best practices to steer you toward a workplace culture that celebrates diversity and fosters inclusivity, ultimately leading to success for all.

Five Rules of Engagement

In the planning, there needs to be outlined rules of engagement to enable a structured progression of where the ideas will take the organization. Here, five rules apply as best practices on the journey:

- **Rule 1: Thorough Understanding**—Show how well you understand the plan and its implications. It is not just about knowledge; it's your chance to demonstrate you've considered the broader context and potential challenges. This won't only make your co-workers and executives trust your initiative, but there will be a confidence that you are well-prepared and have all the skills to handle the proposed changes effectively.
- **Rule 2: Data-Driven Communication**—Executives value information that is concise, relevant, and supported by data. In life, facts are what move people to action. When presenting to higher-level colleagues, focusing on key metrics, real-time analytics, and evidence that directly relate to your proposal is crucial. Don't waste their time with unnecessary information that can slow down the decision-making process. Give them the real deal and never leave out all the pros and cons; that way, they know you're not just selling them some sob story of all the good stuff they know won't fly.
- **Rule 3: Initiative**—Taking initiative is a sign of proactiveness and leadership. Executives appreciate team members who follow instructions, identify improvement opportunities, and take action without waiting for explicit guidance. This demonstrates your commitment to the success of the project or initiative. When Ursula Burns started her career as a summer intern at Xerox, she eventually worked her way up to becoming the company's CEO in 2009. Ursula Burns'

initiative and dedication were instrumental in her rise through the ranks of Xerox. Her leadership and innovative thinking helped steer the company through challenging times, including transitioning into a digital technology and services enterprise. It just shows that initiative can take you far ahead of your co-workers once you are focus-driven.

- **Rule 4: Enthusiasm**—Not only is it infectious, but it can significantly impact how your ideas are received. One notable woman who showed enthusiasm for her initiative and won many over in the fashion industry is Anna Wintour. Since 1988, Anna Wintour has been the editor-in-chief of Vogue magazine and is widely regarded as one of the most influential figures in the fashion world. Her enthusiasm for fashion and keen editorial eye have significantly shaped the industry. When you're genuinely excited about a proposal or project, it energizes you and those around you. It can distinguish between a routine presentation and one that leaves a lasting impression. In fact, people are likely to take the project more seriously than you because there is an aura of passion flowing from how driven you are about the idea's success.

- **Rule 5: Being prepared for questions and potential challenges is a mark of thoroughness**—Nothing should take you by surprise, and executives who see this are more likely to trust your proposal if you've considered various scenarios and have well-thought-out responses to potential queries. It's the demonstration of your dedication to ensuring the success and viability of your plan.

These rules set the stage for having the perfect answers to key questions about your planned goal and the changes you look forward to. Questions like:

- What is the actual goal target of the idea?

- Who are the stakeholders that matter most in planning and executing this idea?
- By projection, what outcome will the idea likely deliver? (The Good, Bad, and Ugly).
- Do I have enough supportive and compelling data to support the plan?
- How can the nature of the data retrieved determine the next steps and measurable outcomes?

Once you align these questions in your planning strategy, then comes the best part. Using the Pyramid Principle!

The Pyramid Principle

Here, you can have an impeccable design laid down with all the data retrieved, the pros and cons in the course of planning, and the desired resolution after all ideas have been sifted and gathered. Let's take, for example, Apple Inc. and discuss one of its many ingenious ideas and how the Pyramid Principle assisted in expanding a situation and revealing the possibilities towards a fallback or a boom in production.

In the early 2000s, Apple Inc. faced a situation where their Macintosh computer sales stagnated, and the company was struggling to gain market share in the PC industry. You can see that in this sample, your first move is to start by explaining the current state or situation; that way, your audience will understand the context and be broad-minded about how it got to this point.

Secondly, highlight the issues or challenges your audience faces in the current situation so they know how invested they must be in the outcome, good or bad. Why do Apple's issues appear more complicated? It was because there was a declining market share, reduced profitability, and a lack of innovation in their product line, and competitors like Microsoft were dominating the market. Everything was evident and glaringly needed the "what next" big idea.

Thirdly, then comes the awaited dawn where a proposed resolution or change that addresses the complications is suggested, and you can just imagine how much that main idea has been long awaited. See how Apple's decision to introduce a series of innovative products changed the situation, starting with the iPod, followed by the iPhone and iPad. These products revolutionized their respective industries and allowed Apple to diversify its product line beyond computers. Good thinking!

By now, you see how the benefits brought about significant change. Apple's revenue and market share skyrocketed, and its value is second to none in the world today with its innovative products that changed how humans interact with technology. The main idea was a success guided by top-notch financial data, stock performance, and customer satisfaction metrics. To make an idea bought and renowned, emphasize the benefits of your proposed resolution by using accurate and compelling data to support your argument and encourage your colleagues to join by showcasing positive outcomes. No one will take your strategy lightly knowing how you have covered all your tracks efficiently.

There is a saying that for every ten men in battle, there is always a traitor, an insider who can sell the team out unless he is found out or won over. The same goes when you have an idea; that's when you should ensure there are no snags to your plans, like people who have all the influence and can use it to tumble your idea into a nightmare. So, to be prepared and not act unaware of potential complications, you should consider:

- **Getting everyone onboard:** Achieving buy-in from all stakeholders can be a significant challenge, both mentally and financially. It's crucial to address the potential resistance to change and allocate resources effectively to overcome these barriers. Ensuring that your corporate inclusion efforts align with organizational goals and values can help mitigate this challenge. You can even engage leadership in discussions about DEI's strategic importance. Use the advantage by sharing industry-specific success stories or case studies highlighting the advantages of diverse and inclusive workplaces. This act of conviction never goes wrong with the right data in hand.

- **Make DEI your culture:** Analyze how DEI principles will be integrated into various aspects of your company's operations, from recruitment and hiring to leadership development and decision-making processes. Just allow diversity and inclusion to be incorporated into training, discussions in affinity groups, and more, and see how people begin embracing the plan like a daily routine never to be missed.

- **Get rid of bias:** Aiming to address unconscious bias in hiring practices is essential because it undermines DEI efforts. Establish different hiring panels or committees to review candidates and make objective decisions. Implement blind recruitment techniques, such as removing identifying information from resumes during initial assessments. Regularly review and update your hiring and promotion criteria to eliminate potential biases. With over 60% of respondents believing their workplaces exhibit bias, it's the perfect moment to recognize these biases and implement training and awareness programs that can help mitigate their impact.

- **Ageism:** Another common bias that can affect the opportunities and experiences of older and younger team members. What does age have to do with service delivery if the job can get done efficiently? When you promote mentorship and reverse mentorship programs, you bridge generational gaps within the workforce. Fostering age-related stereotypes and an age-inclusive environment is essential for DEI success.

- **Sexism:** Once a topic revolves around the male and female sexes, it remains a challenge in many workplaces. There is always a conflicting feeling of who deserves what and when which has affected the smooth working environment. It's time to establish clear guidelines and policies that prohibit gender-based discrimination and provide training to recognize and prevent it. Diversity in leadership roles should be encouraged as this can massively contribute to a more equitable workplace.

- **Halo effect:** Where one's positive traits influence perceptions of their other qualities, leading to bias in decision-making. No good judgment can come from a source when so many people are involved. You need feedback and comments to evaluate and reduce any biased conclusion so employees see the transparency of discussions and objective criteria rather than subjective impressions.

- **Measurement and accountability:** You need precision in providing key performance indicators (KPIs) and metrics to track the progress of your DEI initiatives. Every now and again, analyze data on hiring, promotions, compensation, employee satisfaction, and diversity representation at all levels of the organization. In fact, hold leaders and decision-makers accountable for meeting diversity and inclusion goals and celebrate successes along the way. It keeps everyone, executives and employees, on their toes where DEI is concerned.

Once you have all that covered, it's time to bring home the bacon! Enlighten the employees you've spent time trying to win over about the new culture you want to introduce that will set the company on a different level.

This is when you use the pitching Pyramid Principle.

Pitching

Pitching encompasses best practices and empowers individuals to effectively introduce new concepts, ideas, and policies in the workplace. Mastering this approach enhances pitching skills and boosts the chances of successful implementation. Understand that pitching is fundamental for professionals at all levels, as it allows them to present well-prepared plans and ideas, ultimately bypassing unconscious biases in decision-making processes. To be ahead in the game of pitching means:

1. Ensuring your pitch is clear and easy to understand by using simple language with less jargon or technical terms that your audience may not be familiar with.
2. Crafting a compelling narrative that engages your audience emotionally. Add stories to help people connect and remember your message better.
3. Showing confidence in your idea by speaking with conviction and belief in what you're presenting until it's contagious to your employees.
4. Thoroughly researching your topic and understanding your audience's needs and interests. You should anticipate questions and objections and prepare well-structured responses for whatever comes.
5. Sustaining the interest of your audience throughout the pitch. You can use visuals, AI prompts, anecdotes, and examples to illustrate your points; that way, people are engaged from start to finish.
6. You must be an active listener. Always pay attention to your audience's feedback and adjust your pitch accordingly, showing you value their input and want to get them involved in the process.
7. Being open to criticism and encountering resistance or questions. It doesn't mean the pitch isn't good; it just means you should adapt your pitch to address concerns effectively.
8. Respecting your audience's time by keeping your pitch within the allotted time frame.
9. Using visuals like slides or props to enhance your pitch and make complex information more accessible.

10. Making sure your pitch is relevant to your audience's needs and priorities. Say it tailored, and let your message resonate with them.

11. Following up with your audience after the pitch to address any outstanding questions or concerns. This shows your commitment to the idea.

12. Letting your body language send a compelling message. Maintain eye contact and use gestures purposefully while talking, as your audience will feel at home.

13. Above all, you get to practice your pitch multiple times to refine your delivery and increase your confidence. Rehearse like you would for a performance in front of a trusted colleague or mentor so they give you an honest review.

See how important pitching is? The more you practice, the better you can get at it. Who would have thought that the pyramid principle required this much skill to convince people? In fact, you'll need more than skills; you must have a broader understanding of what the Pyramid Principle truly represents and how it all began.

What Is the Pyramid Principle

In the dynamic era of the 1970s, a remarkable innovator, Barbara Minto, was on a mission to revolutionize the way we communicate complex ideas. For her, great ideas went underexplored because the originators weren't quite there in terms of delivery and conviction. At McKinsey & Company, Barbara was this diligently crafting woman who raised the idea of a technique that would become legendary—the Pyramid Principle.

What was her goal? Barbara aimed to empower consultants and professionals to articulate intricate concepts with clarity. Her visionary work was destined to change how we think about conveying ideas.

Fast-forward to 1987, Barbara Minto's legacy found its voice in the book *The Pyramid Principle: Logic in Writing and Thinking*. There she unveiled the blueprint for structuring information in a way that effortlessly guided even the most intricate ideas from paper to the reader's understanding and appreciation. This became the beginning of a profound shift in communication strategies.

Beyond management consulting, the Pyramid Principle became a versatile tool across diverse businesses, academia, government agencies, and nonprofit organizations. From crafting persuasive business proposals to distilling elaborate strategic plans, the best part is this approach has consistently delivered results. It's so embracing to the point where it's now a powerful cornerstone of effective communication and adequate comprehension of complex concepts.

What most people don't comprehend is that when you apply the Pyramid Principle, you're changing the standard information presentation format where you might start with background information or context and gradually lead up to your main point. The Pyramid Principle causes you to flip that order of expectation by commencing with the most critical message right from the start.

You can call it the "top-down" approach, where the key message is delivered so the audience immediately grasps the central idea without sifting through unnecessary details. Once you've laid out your main point, you then provide supporting information and context using a hierarchical structure. Why does the principle choose to go on this road? That way, your audience will understand the core message, making it easier for them to absorb the context and evidence you provide. They are left with memories of your idea because you shared it with clarity and effectiveness using three memorable steps:

- **Step 1: Impact**—You use compelling and unambiguous statements to set the stage for your entire message. When you initiate your discourse with your main recommendation or answer, you instantly engage your audience and present them with the core message. Think of it as a film director captivating viewers from the very beginning with a gripping scene. The objective is to ensure your primary message takes center stage and hooks your listeners' attention because when you avoid it, the audience gets lost amid an abundance of information.

- **Step 2: Thought-Out Strategy**—To give credence to your idea, substantiate your initial statement with several well-considered supporting arguments that will reinforce your central message and offer context or evidence. You should visualize these arguments as narrative elements in a movie, adding depth and maintaining audience engagement. It's essential that your supporting arguments are spot-on and logically organized. Make them what they should be; a summary of the ideas clustered beneath them that establishes credibility with your audience.

- **Step 3: Foster Trust**—In the ultimate phase, strive to reinforce the trust established by providing data and substantiation to endorse your proposed changes or ideas. Ensure the data enhances the credibility of your message and aids in persuading your audience regarding the validity of your recommendations. This can be like the resolution in a movie plot, where all narrative threads are tied up, leaving the audience convinced and content with how the story ends.

THE PYRAMID PRINCIPLE BLUEPRINT

01

The answer is simply a clear, concise, and effective core message that has four components: **Situation**, **Complication**, **Question**, **Answer**

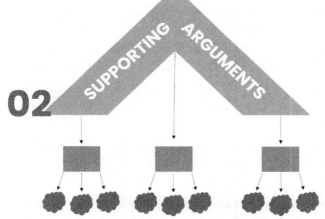

02

Arguments should then be sorted, grouped, and summarized in a logical way; each single thought should be backed by three supporting arguments.

03

Data, evidence, and factual information that validates the supporting arguments

How to Choose a Vision

Once you adhere to these Pyramid steps, you can guarantee that your message resonates clearly and is not eclipsed by biased perspectives or viewpoints. Believe it or not, biased individuals will always rear their heads when you're getting somewhere with new ideas. You will find them even more interested once your idea spurs visionary thinking. This isn't unusual; all companies, organizations, and workers need a vision to achieve similar goals. So, how can you choose one to add to your plan?

1. **Mention Benefits:** Begin your vision by clearly outlining the benefits that your proposed changes will bring. Your executive summary should be concise, powerful, and barrier-free. It's what the famous Dove brand did in their 'Real Beauty' campaign. They emphasized the benefits of promoting realistic beauty standards in the executive summary. Stating how embracing diversity in beauty leads to increased consumer trust and brand loyalty. This initial step sets the tone for the entire vision, ensuring that it grabs attention and communicates the brand's intentions effectively.

2. **Have Shared Future Vision:** Promote inclusivity and encourage everyone within your organization to contribute to this vision. A shared vision not only aligns with DEI principles but also encourages collaboration and buy-in from various stakeholders.

3. **Align with Core Values:** Identify your company's core values, but also be open to evolving them if needed by seeking input from colleagues. You'll find and understand which values resonate with them and align with the envisioned future. This collaborative approach ensures your vision is firmly rooted in the organization's identity and purpose. Look what Athleta and The Body Shop stand for today; they combine their core values with environmental

sustainability, inclusivity, and ethical behavior so customers and employees can enjoy a sense of confidence, respect, and social responsibility all in the world that's passionate about ageless beauty. The message here is what will make women convinced about the brands.

4. **Simplify Your Values:** In a world of information overload, try staying simple. Keep your values human, straightforward, realistic, and easily recallable. Clarity is essential to ensure that your vision is not only understood but also embraced by all employees, regardless of their role or level within the organization. In 2011, When Patagonia, a clothing company, ran a full-page advertisement in The New York Times with a bold headline that read, "Don't Buy This Jacket" on a Black Friday, they had a mission. They were featuring one of their best-selling products, a down jacket. The aim was to explain the environmental impact of the jacket's production, from the resources used to its carbon footprint, so that consumers would consider the environmental consequences of their purchases. The core value here was to show the world that they were a company that stood for integrity by prioritizing the planet over profit. Smart way to convince an audience, wouldn't you say?

5. **Seek New Values:** Building on what already exists is a powerful way to maintain continuity while evolving. Additionally, actively seeking new values that reflect the changing landscape of your organization and the world so you don't seem obsolete in the eyes of your audience is a nice way to stay in the game and make a difference. Don't just collect all inputs because they are available; let them come from a diverse group of team members to ensure that your vision remains fresh, relevant, and up-to-date.

6. **Filter and Refine:** Stitch Fix, co-founded by Katrina Lake, underwent a process of filtering and refining its values to align with its mission of personal styling. They refined values like "Client-Centric" to emphasize their dedication to

providing personalized fashion experiences. It's all about prioritizing values that best represent your organization's goals and aspirations and filtering out values that may be less relevant or conflicting. A refined vision with a focused set of values allows for a clear and impactful message that resonates deeply with your team.

Now, armed with your well-thought-out plans and innovative ideas, you're perfectly poised to inspire your audience to embark on crafting a powerful business plan. This plan can take the form of a dynamic spreadsheet or an engaging slideshow, delving into your present circumstances, the hurdles you face, and the ingenious solutions you've conceived. While certain sections may be a work in progress, infusing them with initial data-driven insights is a fantastic way to get started. Consider this as the spark that ignites the flame of motivation, the first step towards creating a comprehensive framework. You can further refine and develop this foundation in the chapters that lie ahead. So, go ahead, and take a look! Your journey to success begins here.

Ensure your strategy remains accessible as forthcoming tactics guide you to fill every facet of your presentation board or slideshow. Now, in the next chapter, uncover the principles of initiation and learn how to rally all aboard the DEI journey to spark up transformative shifts.

4

HOW TO NURTURE A CURIOUS INCEPTION MINDSET TO WELCOME CHANGE

All of us do not have equal talent, but all of us should have an equal
opportunity to develop our talents.
—*John F. Kennedy (Kennedy J.F, 1964)*

The DEI LightHouse Strategy

Before the world tilted toward the hunger of ensuring an environment that's inclusive and conscious of all, irrespective of human factors, everything was almost sedentary. People appreciate only those they know and don't feel the need to be open to encountering new people, places, or activities. For them, the more was never the merrier; instead, that was a case of chaotic living that caused things to go topsy-turvy. This was the mindset, and it felt good and acceptable, but was it enough?

Of course not. With the dawning of migration and crosscultural interrelations, the DEI became the next best choice to help more work environments experience innovative ideas. At this point, it's widely recognized that implementing training programs and workshops is crucial in fostering a DEI mindset and ensuring organizations stay firmly committed to upholding a culture of diversity and inclusion. In fact, a staggering 92% of business leaders concur that a strategic workforce education initiative should serve as the catalyst for achieving their diversity and inclusion objective (InStride, 2021). This is good, but many more things are involved that bring the DEI Light-House Strategy initiative to play.

The DEI LightHouse Strategy doesn't just believe in making robust plans and pitching them with style and precision; they are all about accountability and investment.

One of the DEI LightHouse Strategies, "Define Vision, Purpose, and Values," compels employers to set a compelling DEI vision aligned with their broader mission. It entails defining core values centered on fairness, respect, and transparency and actively engaging leadership to garner support. Employee involvement in shaping the vision and values is paramount. Transparent communication, backed by education, ensures that everyone understands the significance of DEI. Measurable goals and accountability mechanisms must be established, alongside a commitment to reviewing and adapting policies. External engagement broadens the scope of impact. A continuous improvement mindset underscores this strategy, as organizations continually aim to foster inclusivity and equity.

For instance, in the case of Lighthouse Corporation, this strategy was implemented by creating a robust DEI vision statement that emphasized the company's commitment to diversity and inclusion. This vision was reinforced by a set of core values, which were integrated into the corporate culture. Leadership buy-in was achieved through targeted workshops, and employees played a pivotal role in refining the vision. Regular training sessions ensured that all staff members were well-informed, and metrics were implemented to assess progress and hold leadership accountable. Lighthouse also actively engaged with external organizations and stakeholders to advance its DEI goals, creating a more inclusive workplace environment over time.

To effectively utilize this strategy, as a leader or a manager, start by defining specific, measurable, and time-bound goals for DEI within your organization. These goals should align with your broader mission and values, ensuring everyone understands the significance of these objectives. Next, make strategic investments in DEI initiatives that support your goals. This may include training programs, mentorship opportunities, or initiatives to promote diversity in hiring and leadership positions. It's essential to allocate resources and budget to these efforts; it's your way of showing commitment to driving change.

Believe it or not, accountability is a crucial component of this strategy. Hold yourself and your leadership team responsible for meeting the established DEI goals. Regularly review progress, collect data, and communicate results transparently to all stakeholders. Engage with external organizations and stakeholders to gain additional insights and promote broader change within your industry. Create a comprehensive DEI plan to ensure everyone in your organization understands, accepts, and embraces these changes. This plan should include strategies for educating employees at all levels, fostering an inclusive culture, and addressing bias and discrimination when they occur. By providing ongoing education and training, you empower your workforce to participate in the transformation process actively.

Additionally, encourage employees to share their visions, goals, and statements related to DEI. This collaborative approach can lead to a more inclusive and diverse workplace, as it incorporates a variety of perspectives and experiences. Furthermore, highlight the benefits of these changes, such as improved employee morale, creativity, and productivity, in your proposal to gain widespread support.

How to Control Biases

This is not to say that you can easily evade certain biases and reservations during your planning because you can't. For most managers and leaders, biases are ingrained in how they strategize, and connect, and becoming more aware and prepared for this takes a lot of steps.

1. **Awareness of Biases:** Always recognizing that the presence of unconscious biases is the foundational step in addressing them, which involves acknowledging that everyone, regardless of their background or intentions, may hold biases. This self-awareness encourages individuals to examine their beliefs, attitudes, and behaviors critically. It's essential to understand that biases can manifest in various forms, such as racial, gender, age, or cognitive biases.

2. **Unconscious Bias Training:** It's a program that is important in bridging the gap between awareness and action. They provide individuals with the knowledge and tools to identify and manage their biases. Effective training modules delve into the science behind bias, emphasizing that it is a natural part of human cognition. Such programs empower individuals to challenge their biases and make fairer decisions by fostering empathy and understanding.

3. **Unpacking Unconscious Biases:** When it comes to unconscious biases, there is a wide range of stereotypes, prejudices, and discriminatory behaviors. It's vital to delve deeper into these biases to comprehend their effects on individuals and organizations. By examining specific scenarios and real-world examples, you can grasp how biases influence everyday interactions, affecting everything from hiring decisions to employee morale. This deeper understanding serves as a motivator for change.

4. **Organizational Improvement:** Addressing unconscious bias is not solely an individual endeavor but a collective responsibility. Organizations must foster a culture of inclusion and diversity where everyone feels valued and heard. This involves leadership commitment, policies promoting equity, and inclusive recruitment, retention, and advancement practices. Employees at all levels should actively contribute to building an environment free from bias and discrimination.

5. **Efficacy of Training Programs:** Organizations should regularly assess the impact of their unconscious bias training initiatives. This involves tracking changes in attitudes and behaviors and monitoring key metrics related to diversity, equity, and inclusion. Feedback mechanisms, surveys, and follow-up assessments can help refine and improve training programs.

Recall that in sharing details of training and its effectiveness, each form of bias training serves the crucial purpose of addressing specific prejudices and stereotypes, fostering an inclusive work environment, and promoting fairness and equity among all employees. With various bias training programs, organizations can create a more comprehensive approach to tackling unconscious biases and promoting diversity and inclusion.

Trainings Focussed on Bias Control

- **Gender bias training** addresses prejudices and stereotypes related to gender, promoting equality and fair treatment of individuals regardless of gender identity. Being a woman or a man should have no base in determining the execution of any duties as long as it gets done efficiently.
- **Racial bias training** focuses on confronting and mitigating biases related to race and ethnicity. It emphasizes the importance of treating people equitably, irrespective of their racial background. Your ethnicity is a pride you should carry everywhere, whether it shows in how you dress or the speaking phonetics you possess.
- **LGBTQ bias training** aims to create a more inclusive workplace for individuals of diverse sexual orientations and gender identities. You get educated about the challenges faced by LGBTQ+ individuals, which fosters empathy and ensures that the work environment is welcoming and respectful.

- **Age bias training** addresses stereotypes and biases related to age, ensuring that older and younger employees are treated fairly and respectfully. After all, it is said that age is nothing but a number and that there should be no limit to how much a person can deliver in duties. Room is and should always be made for all.
- **Disability bias training** raises awareness about prejudices faced by individuals with disabilities and promotes a more accessible and inclusive work environment.
- **Religious bias training** helps employees recognize and confront biases based on religious beliefs. Here, you learn to appreciate the importance of accommodating diverse religious practices and not favoring one religious group over another.
- **Lookism bias training** targets biases related to physical appearance, challenging stereotypes that may affect hiring, promotions, or workplace interactions. It encourages a more inclusive perspective by highlighting that individuals should be assessed based on their qualifications and skills rather than their appearance.
- **Lesser-known bias training** covers many biases that may not be as widely recognized as others. These biases can include biases related to socioeconomic status, personality type (e.g., extrovert vs. introvert), and communication style. If you're interested in how upper class a person is before giving room to their ideas or how worthy an organization is to have your ingenious idea, there can be a problem. Also, if someone prefers to stay more reclusive, that shouldn't be an issue of concern; instead, addressing these biases will foster a more inclusive and accepting workplace.

Diversity and Inclusion Trainings

Every training that must be worthwhile and exciting can occur in many ways. The easiest way is to have individuals do a one-on-one interactive online session, allowing swift communication of ideas from anywhere. But that's not all:

- **Unconscious Bias Online Training:** This method has gained popularity due to its scalability and accessibility. In today's digital age, it's a practical way to reach a geographically dispersed workforce. All you need to do is make it interactive, engaging, and tailored to various learning styles, making them essential tools for raising awareness about unconscious biases. However, organizations should complement online training with real-life discussions and applications to ensure the lessons translate into tangible behavior change.

- **Diversity Training Programs:** Encouraging employees to participate in diversity training programs demonstrates a commitment to inclusivity. It's a proactive step that sets the tone for the organization's culture. When employees see leadership endorsing these programs, they are more likely to engage willingly. You should offer programs to accommodate different learning preferences and address specific diversity and inclusion challenges within the organization so no topic area is displaced.

- **Awareness Training:** If you are the foundation for any meaningful diversity and inclusion initiative, you would understand that awareness training is akin to turning on the lights in a dark room. Without awareness, biases remain hidden, so leaders and managers should view this training as a starting point rather than a final destination. Following up with more targeted training and practical applications of diversity principles is crucial to drive lasting change.

- **Basic Diversity Training:** There is nothing more promising in training than having all participants share a common language of diversity. The vocabulary and understanding of diversity and inclusion concepts align the workforce with the organization's diversity goals. It won't only keep this training engaging and relevant, but it will avoid a one-size-fits-all approach.

- **Skill-Based Diversity Training:** While awareness is vital, skill-based training takes it further by equipping employees with practical skills. Effective communication, conflict resolution, and teamwork in diverse settings are critical skills for the modern workplace. Skill-based training empowers employees to navigate complex situations and contribute positively to diverse teams.

- **Diversity Audit Training:** Diversity audits provide valuable insights into an organization's strengths and weaknesses in the diversity and inclusion arena. You can think of it as an analytic of DEI where, with the data retrieved, training key personnel becomes authenticated and ensures the audit is conducted thoroughly and impartially. It also underscores the organization's commitment to transparency and continuous improvement as attention is given to all loopholes that need covering and smoothening.

- **Intermediate Diversity Training:** Diversity is a multifaceted topic that delves into deeper discussions, exploring intersectionality, privilege, and allyship. Such training encourages participants to think critically about diversity issues and fosters a culture of ongoing learning and growth. With these parameters, you can feel free and open to discuss any area of DEI, especially those that seem ignored and overlooked for fear of sensitivity.

- **Mobile Learning:** Know the power and swiftness at which mobile technology is taking over in providing ease of communication and a practical solution for organizations with remote or globally distributed teams. It aligns with the changing dynamics of work, where flexibility and remote work are becoming increasingly prevalent. Mobile training ensures all employees can access essential diversity training materials regardless of location.

You can see excellent diversity training opportunities, and inclusion isn't left out. However, training demands time and money, and with a reasonable budget, **inclusion training** is another beneficial option with great potential for an action plan for change.

Inclusive training takes on a more educational approach designed to foster a sense of belonging and respect for all individuals, regardless of their background, abilities, or perspectives. **Why does it matter?** Because it creates a workplace environment where employees feel valued and empowered to contribute their best. Inclusive training not only ticks the diversity box; it actively promotes diversity, equity, and inclusion (DEI) as essential organizational values. It boosts workplace morale by creating a culture of respect and collaboration, improving job satisfaction and overall well-being.

What Are the Benefits?

McKinsey & Co. (2023) found that companies with more diverse executive teams are 25–36% more likely to have above-average profitability. This data underscores the business case for inclusive training as much more than morals, but also reaping the tangible benefits of a diverse and inclusive workforce in productivity and retention. Diverse teams bring a more comprehensive range of perspectives and ideas, which can lead to more innovative solutions and better decision-making.

Another benefit is perspective-taking. It's a valuable training module that encourages employees to step into the shoes of their colleagues from diverse backgrounds. It's a powerful empathy-building exercise that fosters understanding and reduces biases. When your mind is too joggled to consider different viewpoints and experiences of other employees besides yourself, empathy and open-mindedness come into play, contributing to a more inclusive workplace. Suggesting such modules for free or low-cost training can be a cost-effective way to enhance diversity and inclusion. For instance, two co-workers, Michelle and Sally, disagree during a team meeting because Sally believes Michelle constantly interrupts her repeatedly during her presentation. Using a perspective-taking exercise, each employee is asked to switch roles and see the situation from the other's point of view.

Guess what happens?

In Michelle's role, Sally realizes the interruption was out of excitement to share her ideas. On the other hand, Michelle understands how frustrating it can be to have someone interrupt during a presentation and recognizes the need to be more mindful of it in the future. Both employees gain empathy for each other's perspectives, leading to improved communication and a more harmonious working relationship.

"I am, but I'm not" is another effective and free training exercise that encourages participants to reflect on their identities and the unique aspects of their personalities. You are prompted to recognize that people are multifaceted, with many dimensions to their identities. This exercise can be eye-opening, helping employees appreciate the complexity of diversity beyond visible characteristics. It fosters a sense of unity by acknowledging our shared humanity and individuality.

Morgan: *"I am an extrovert, but I'm not always the life of the party."*

Shirley: *"I am introverted, but I'm not anti-social; I enjoy deep one-on-one conversations."*

Carlo: *"I am a parent, but I'm not always available outside of work hours."*

Priya: *"I am young, but I'm not inexperienced; I bring fresh ideas to the team."*

Everyone identifies with a trait and isn't ashamed to make it known so there is an understanding among themselves.

Equity Training

This brings us to the final destination of the journey: equity. As straightforward as it might sound, equity is another initiative that would do well with the help of training that establishes its meaning and how it is a means to an end where DEI is of note. Regarding employment equity online training, you are guaranteed one of the most valuable resources primarily designed for HR professionals and those in leadership positions. If you want to address issues relating to workplace employment equity by making it a comprehensive but straightforward subject, this training is all you need. It includes in-depth modules on understanding employment equity legislation, creating equitable workplace policies, and implementing strategies to achieve a diverse and inclusive workforce. Not to mention the ease at which HR professionals and leaders can access crucial information that is up-to-date with the latest regulations and best practices. It also provides a platform for interactive learning, enabling participants to engage in discussions, ask questions, and share insights with colleagues.

If there is one thing that makes online training worthwhile, it's the convenience to busy employees who need the flexibility to complete the course and also the real-life case studies and practical examples that illustrate the impact of employment equity on organizations. With these scenarios, HR professionals and leaders grasp the significance of DEI in the workplace. When workers know there is no pressure to finish a course because of the first interest in comprehension and application, it enhances their knowledge and skills in employment equity.

This training is an essential resource for all staff members within an organization because it is designed to provide a foundational understanding of employment equity principles and practices. Here, you will find topics such as the legal framework surrounding employment equity, the importance of diversity in the workplace, and strategies for promoting equity and inclusion.

Another key benefit of the training is its accessibility to all employees, regardless of their role or level within the organization. You get to appreciate the organization's commitment to creating an equitable workplace and its role in supporting these efforts, thereby leaving room for questions and concerns relating to DEI to be adequately responded to in the most professional fashion. Organizations can create a shared understanding of the value of diversity and inclusion by equipping staff with basic employment equity knowledge. This, in turn, contributes to a more harmonious and productive workplace. Basic training can also serve as a foundation for more specialized equity training for HR professionals and leadership.

Checklist of Key Employment Equity Facts

Designing a brief checklist of key employment equity facts helps educate colleagues and garner their support for equity initiatives. When you have details like the purpose of employment equity, its legal framework, and its role in promoting fairness and justice in the workplace, employees will be clear as to how passionate the organization is about an equitable workforce.

Note that the purpose of employment equity is threefold:

1. To redress past discrimination
2. To promote equal opportunities for all
3. To eliminate employment barriers that perpetuate inequality

By sharing this fundamental understanding, organizations can emphasize their commitment to social justice and inclusivity. With a checklist, employees can now demystify employment equity, where the topical engagement is no longer restricted but open to dialogues and reviews. It can be a conversation starter that encourages employees to ask questions, seek clarification, and actively participate in equity-related initiatives within the organization.

Remember that establishing a strong groundwork for transformation and initiation will never be easy but stimulates a more inclusive and harmonious workplace across all dimensions. While it might entail some expenses, it stands as an indispensable component of your proposal or concrete reforms. Now, you can go a step ahead in creating a unique checklist and, while at it, look into how vital it is to use these pragmatic approaches for seamlessly integrating DEI principles into your day-to-day workplace operations. Chapter five has so much more to tell you.

YOUR FEEDBACK IS VALUABLE!

You're halfway through "Impactful Inclusive Leadership," and I'd love to hear your thoughts. Your feedback not only helps me but also fellow leaders seeking valuable insights.

It's simple to leave a review on Amazon: Visit the book's Amazon 'Write a customer review' page by clicking the link or scanning the code below.

By sharing your experience, you're contributing to a community of leaders helping each other thrive. Your words of wisdom can inspire and guide them, making their journey smoother and more fulfilling.

Your insights matter – thank you for being part of my journey!

5

THE ACT OF MARRYING CULTURAL DIFFERENCES AND IDEAS

Diversity is the art of thinking independently together.
——Malcolm Forbes (Teambuilding, 2022)

The Lighthouse Impact

Have you ever considered the remarkable advantages of diversity in the workplace once you begin to actualize your plans? It's a powerful catalyst for success. As diverse companies are 70% more likely to seize new market opportunities (Hewitt et al., 2013), you will also find that diverse teams are 87% more inclined to make decisions that not only benefit the company but also enrich the lives of everyone involved (Sucich K., 2022). To make headway to seeing these benefits come to life, you must by now identify the journey so far in instilling the DEI strategy.

In the Lighthouse model introduced in an earlier chapter, what outcomes were derived from applying that approach? Have you been able to envision the right practical tools and strategies that will make DEI much more than a culture? With answers to these questions, you will feel ready to enter the fourth stage of the DEI Lighthouse framework.

It's a framework that highlights the remarkable success in the realm of DEI achieved in 2023. The Lighthouse organizations have set the standard by not only recognizing DEI as a priority but also by actively designing innovative solutions to address DEI challenges within their workplaces. A standout example of their impactful initiatives is the implementation of a comprehensive leadership development program in India. This was one of the many testament to their commitment to fostering diversity and inclusion in the workplace, particularly in a region where such efforts are crucial. Beyond geographical boundaries, Lighthouse has shown its desire for global engagement, thereby underscoring the universality of DEI's importance. So, as you progress in developing your plan, recognize especially the insights gained from these leading organizations, as they can serve as a solid foundation for your own DEI proposal.

Best Strategies to Ensure DEI

Imagine you hold a powerful position of making life-changing decisions for your company in hiring, firing, and promoting; what would be the best strategies to ensure DEI plays its part in the outcomes of your resolutions?

1. **Recruitment Process Overhaul:** Conventional recruitment approaches may unintentionally exhibit bias towards particular groups. In such moments, leaders should contemplate a comprehensive reform of these processes to ensure equity and inclusiveness. Embracing novel strategies and methodologies can broaden the talent spectrum, thus enhancing diversity in the pool of potential candidates. No need for the old ways of being straight jacket when you can give room for broader perspectives by being open and less stereotyped.

2. **Welcome Ideas:** Fostering diversity requires leaders to inspire employees to value different viewpoints and backgrounds. Implementing training initiatives, such as exercises that encourage considering other perspectives, can aid employees in recognizing the constraints of their ideas and becoming more receptive to the ideas of others. In fact, you might consider combining ideas to create a holistic perspective that will meet the company's needs extensively.

3. **Retention Measures for Diverse Talent:** Potent recruitment and advancement strategies should be supplemented with robust retention measures. If you don't feel like you're growing, then the work can never seem worth your time and years. Progression goes beyond high pay but a rising career, and leaders should guarantee the celebration and dissemination of success stories from individuals of diverse backgrounds to motivate others. When you encounter top executives from all backgrounds who rose through the ranks in wealth and career, it spurs you for job success.

4. **Acknowledge Cultural differences:** There cannot be a more joyous time to appreciate culture and rejoice in disparities within the workplace than now. Not only have cultural differences nurtured a feeling of belonging and mutual esteem among employees, but it has also coopted a sense of festivities in various ways. Organizations now introduce the observance of cultural occasions and disseminate accomplishments and triumphs from diverse employees. They even go the length of establishing a long trail of the success journey of these employees to show how their differences never stopped their successes. An inspiration to all and a backbone to the future of DEI strategies.

5. **Diversify Teams:** Diversity should extend beyond just entry-level personnel and encompass teams engaged in various projects and endeavors. The selection of employees from diverse age groups, racial backgrounds, and genders for project teams serves as a safeguard against the domination of

discussions by a single, uniform perspective. When you go to watch the Super Bowl, there are no age limits to who enjoys the game; it's a combination of all, and that's what DEI aims to achieve long term.

6. **Who is your Diversity Expert?** Leaders should contemplate the recruitment of a Chief Inclusion Officer or an adept specialist tasked with ongoing evaluation of the organization's diversity endeavors. With them on board, updates on the highs and lows of DEI are always brought forward for assessment and next steps. You bring professionals who are proficient in conducting an exhaustive analysis of diversity within the organization, and you are sure to get invaluable, data-centric insight to guide decision-making. Can you picture having someone like Dr. Johnnetta B. Cole, former president of Spelman College and Bennett College and renowned diversity expert on the organizational board of directors? Her work in academia and beyond has contributed significantly to promoting diversity and inclusion, so think how her input will leave an indelible mark on the company's DEI transformation system. It's an approach that can't be overlooked by any leader who wants to see their DEI practice tools make meaning.

7. **Check Leadership Diversity:** Leaders should assess the diversity within their leadership teams. Is there adequate representation from various demographic groups? These questions help evaluate the system, identify gaps in diversity, and inform the need for further recruitment efforts in alignment with equity-focused strategies. It's a big step toward creating an inclusive culture. When you feel like you're working with a team of executives who are more male than female or more 40+ than their late 20s, it can be the best time to bring in a diversity expert to level the ground and set the stage for a profiting DEI strategy.

8. **Empower Multilingual Workforce:** Once you embrace a multilingual workforce, rest assured that your organization

will have employees eager to speak multiple languages and share discussions on cultural disparities to foster better relationships and an inclusive environment. A place where language barriers are reduced, and individuals from diverse linguistic backgrounds feel valued, heard, and appreciated because they bring something unique and possibly unfamiliar to the floor. If you're smart about the benefits of DEI, you can use this approach to create culturally sensitive marketing campaigns where employees connect with customers from diverse linguistic backgrounds. As a result, they will expand the company's market reach and increase customer loyalty. It's called thinking out of the box.

9. **Enforce Anti-Discriminatory Policies:** The implementation and strict enforcement of anti-discriminatory policies are essential in creating an inclusive environment. Policies that will set the tone for respecting individual differences and promoting equality. They create a sense of fairness and establish a foundation for an inclusive culture. No one will experience the look of snivelry or riddle knowing that there are laws governing against such.

10. **Engage Focus Groups:** The use of focus groups and gatherings of like-minded individuals can be a valuable strategy for gaining insights and facilitating open, honest discussions on diversity and inclusion topics. Focus groups provide a platform for employees to share their experiences, perspectives, and suggestions for improvement, enhancing understanding and promoting inclusion. It's like having college students discussing with their faculty heads issues of bullying caused by discrimination and having the victims share their fears and the way forward. There can't be a more constructive conversation than this, as it will give the group a chance to see DEI with a keener eye.

Focus Groups

The best part about the focus group is that it's open to all, young and old, employees and employers. Everyone has the unique opportunity to embrace DEI in the workplace in many ways. It can be:

- **Celebrate Cultural Diversity:** Start by embracing traditions and encouraging employees to share their culture, festivals, and practices. Celebrate these diverse occasions within the workplace to foster inclusivity and understanding. There can be special ways to mark occasions through cultural food feasts and dances, allowing some employees to mark their international days in their own ways, possibly by wearing their native wears and more. You can also offer cultural awareness and sensitivity training to educate employees about different cultures and traditions, promoting respect, curiosity, and a stronger mutual and working relationship. Also, leaders might contemplate providing employees with the option to choose a specific number of holidays, even if the company doesn't officially recognize them. This allows them to take time off to celebrate their cultural observances, such as Yom Kippur, Diwali, and others, while still receiving personal paid leave.
- **Promote Inclusive Communication:** If you have the discipline of active listening, it can make people appreciate your sense of empathy and eagerness to help others and give room for all. This is what inclusion is all about in the workplace. In meetings and discussions, ensure everyone's voice is heard before decisions are made. There is the confidence it gives employees knowing they're free to express their likes and dislikes, and it won't reflect on their position or employer's opinion of them. Alternatively, for those who are shy or uncomfortable, establish anonymous feedback mechanisms so they can express their opinions without fear of retribution, encouraging open dialogue.

- **Stimulate Innovative Thinking:** When a team is allowed to think more diversely by including individuals with various perspectives, experiences, and backgrounds, you will find that the problem-solving approach will be less one-track-minded and more encompassing. The more avenues there are for workshops on creativity and innovation, the greater the chances of innovative thinking and unique insights coming to the table.

- **Personalizing Connections:** Employees should be encouraged to have connective conversations with their employers and colleagues on a personal level. A sense of belonging and camaraderie through mentoring circles is always a welcome way to strengthen growth-oriented conversations that will let employees know there is a place to get valuable support and meaningful connections.

- **Cross-Cultural Collaborations:** With global exchange programs or overseas assignments where employees use communication platforms like Teams, Slack, and Webex to share business ideas and discuss the latest global changes, there can be a diverse work environment culture even from a mile away. Such experiences broaden perspectives and enhance global understanding of issues as these employees speak from their encounters with the economic situation within their confines all under an organization. If you have seen journalists share conference meetings about global issues and the approach toward broadcast, that is a reflection of DEI at work in the workplace.

- Inclusive Hiring Practices: Begin by unleashing the power of Diverse Talent from the get-go of recruitment. Don't just check boxes to show you have met hiring requirements, recognizing the importance and value of having diverse hands on board. Candidates' different life experiences can spark innovation, creativity, and unique problem-solving. So, when you revamp your hiring practices to welcome diversity, you know you're opening the door to a world of possibilities.

- **Respectful Communication:** There is a saying that respect is reciprocal, and it is so true. Once there is equal and respectful dialogue every now and again, it's the cornerstone of any inclusive workplace. It's not just about what you say but how you say it. Being mindful of how your words and actions affect others, regardless of their background, shows you are sensitive to people's feelings and demeanor. When you and the colleague next to you decide to contribute equally and respectfully to conversations, the workplace becomes a more harmonious and productive environment.
- **Leverage Employee Resource Groups:** By now, you should be familiar with the benefits of Unity and Growth within ERGs and how they offer a unique space for connection and learning. These groups are instrumental in broadening engagements and expression to eye-opening experiences, helping everyone appreciate colleagues' challenges, triumphs, and aspirations from various backgrounds. It's a chance to stand together and work toward shared goals.
- **Learning and Expanding Diversity Horizons:** Personal growth through education is a journey. When you dedicate time to learning about different cultures, traditions, and perspectives, you enrich your life and ability to support and appreciate diversity. It's a commitment to lifelong learning that benefits both individuals and the workplace. You will learn to meet people halfway whenever they are slow to comprehend due to language or act in a certain way due to cultural background. Nothing will come as a surprise or discomfort. Instead, you become more accommodating in a diverse workplace, knowing there is something unique about everyone.
- **Be the Change You Wish to See:** Once you treat others as you want to be treated, this golden rule becomes the fundamental principle for which you promote DEI as an activist and an employee. Beyond being a workplace practice, it should be a way of life where we set the tone for

an inclusive and respectful environment. It's a personal commitment to be the change we wish to see in the world, one interaction at a time.

Activities to Promote DEI in the Workplace

You will find a range of activities that not only promote diverse thinking and acceptance in the workplace but also infuse a sense of fun and engagement into the process. Nothing too serious, just some exercises designed to create a personal connection among colleagues by introducing a more inclusive and understanding work environment. Once you explore these activities, you'll discover how each one can contribute to a workplace that values diversity and celebrates differences while ensuring that everyone's voice is heard and appreciated.

Here is how you can get started:

Activity 1: The Shape of Others

Here, develop empathy by understanding the factors that have shaped your colleagues' perspectives over the years to this point. Everyone shares a personal object or memento that represents a significant event or aspect of their background. This highlights the unique qualities that each person brings to the team.

Instructions

- Create small groups of colleagues, possibly five or ten each.
- Get each participant to share the key life experiences and influences that have shaped their beliefs and viewpoints. Could be cultural background, upbringing, personal experiences, or role models.
- Encourage active listening, and questions and answers sessions to understand each person's unique journey better.
- Afterward, reconvene as a larger group and discuss the eye-opening moments and insights gained from this activity.

Activity 2: The Rose and the Thorn Exchange

Let employees share successes and struggles, a combination of the positive and negative aspects of their professional or personal lives. It will build trust and understanding and deepen empathy and solidarity.

Instructions

- Begin by sitting in a circle and taking turns sharing both a "rose" (a personal or professional success) and a "thorn" (a challenge or adversity) you've faced.
- Celebrate achievements spoken of and create empathy and understanding for the obstacles others may have encountered.
- Above all, focus on active listening and providing support to colleagues sharing their stories. There could be teary moments, and it's a sign that progress is being made and people are beginning to get intentional about honest reveals.

Activity 3: Confronting Stereotypes

Challenge and deconstruct stereotypes by opening a discourse on biases. There is no shame in discussing what mindset you have about a certain person's ideology and having it demystified in open dialogues. Ever heard of "Inclusion Starts With I"? Accenture, a professional services company, developed this program for employees so they could take a self-assessment to explore their own biases and learn how to promote a more inclusive workplace. This activity has been instrumental in sustaining DEI and debunking prejudices that can be found in the workplace.

Instructions

- Prepare a list of common stereotypes or biases related to different groups or backgrounds. What do you think about a certain mode of dressing or eating of a particular culture and lay it on the table for discussion?

- With that stereotype stated, in pairs or small groups, participants take turns drawing each stereotype from a hat and discussing their personal experiences or insights related to that stereotype. Where have they witnessed it or been confronted concerning it?

- Someone from the group who belongs to the school of thought surrounding that stereotype can give clarity about it. Then, to encourage open dialogue about the impact of stereotypes and how they can be harmful, the stereotype is presented with a better understanding from an authentic source.

- It's all with the goal of debunking myths and empowering participants to challenge stereotypes when they encounter them rather than using them for office gossip and poor judgment.

Activity 4: The Shoe Swap

When you put yourself in someone else's shoes, you learn empathy in the most personal way, and that is the whole idea behind this exercise. Google performed this exercise once, where they had colleagues switch roles for a period of time just so everyone could get a feel of what working in another department was like. Everyone got a taste of their coworkers' workspace, the joys, and pains, and there was more appreciation among them. The mode of making it worthwhile can be by:

Instructions

- First, ask participants to pair up with a colleague from a different background or perspective, and it should be someone they are unfamiliar with and whose departmental responsibilities are alien to them. It creates room for curiosity and excitement.

- Then, the show switching begins with their partner for a set period. Each person attempts to experience the world from their partner's perspective and encounters with clients, leaders, and coworkers.
- Afterward, the period elapses, and partners discuss their experiences, what they learned, and how it felt to walk in someone else's shoes, especially if they believed their partner's responsibilities were a walk in the park. At this point, there will be an opinion change and an appreciation of what everyone does in the workplace, no matter how little.

Activity 5: Bias Awareness

The impact of bias in the workplace will continually be treated with kid gloves unless more awareness programs are introduced concerning it and how to streamline it best. More exposure to bias and discrimination can be a great start, and it doesn't always need to feel serious or uptight. It can be in the form of games and activities involving bias and diversity. By playing out these scenarios, employees gain a deeper understanding of how to promote inclusivity in the workplace.

Instructions

- Share thought-provoking articles, videos, or stories about diversity and inclusion with your colleagues.
- Let employees reflect on the content and its implications so they know how much damage can be caused by bias and how impactful DEI can be to dispel these negatives.
- Host a group discussion where everyone shares their thoughts, insights, and any actions they plan to take after gaining new perspectives. What they would like to do differently moving forward would be a great way to start.

If you really want to feel at home with diversity at play, see it as a gateway to boundless innovations and unbridled creativity. A way of unlocking a world of untapped potential and unique viewpoints where you not only accept but celebrate the differences, recognizing that each person brings their own set of experiences and insights to the table. It's these diverse thoughts and talents that have the power to elevate your organization to new heights. But, it takes more than mere acceptance; you must also actively work on creating an equitable environment. Equity isn't just a buzzword; it's the foundation for a fair and just workplace. When everyone is given equal opportunities and support, this, in turn, fuels collaboration, and overall job satisfaction. Your plan's success hinges on these interconnected principles of DEI working together harmoniously. So, embark on this journey of transformation, where diverse thinking and equitable practices become the cornerstones of your organization's success.

INVITE SKILLS, INNOVATION, AND ACHIEVEMENT

Too many of us still believe our differences define us.
—John Lewis (Teambuilding, 2022)

The Opportunistic Equity Method

I t's obvious to see the fruitfulness of DEI so far and the lagging effect for organizations who have taken it trivially over the years. Hope is not lost, and adding to these findings, there has been an opportunistic equity strategy where equal chances are offered to employees seeking to rise in their careers and gain earned promotions. It's why equity isn't just another strategy to encourage commitment and reward for hard work; it's a means to reveal how there should be a level playing ground for all employees.

In 2019, the National Center for Education Statistics showed a significant disparity in access to training programs among racial and ethnic groups. African Americans and Hispanics were revealed to be more likely to enroll in such programs, which may stem from the challenges they face due to lower graduation rates and limited opportunities. The statistics underscore education's pivotal role in shaping future earning potential, as a Bachelor's degree can translate to an additional $400,000 in lifetime earnings. This stark economic reality serves as a compelling motivator for individuals from minority groups to advocate for equitable access to education and career advancement opportunities. It clearly indicates that underrepresented communities increasingly recognize the importance of standing up for their rights and demanding more inclusive and equitable workplaces and educational environments (Instride, 2021).

So, what really constitutes the essence of equity in the workplace? Is it just about having everyone get fair-share in everything as long as they have earned it? It could be, or there is so much more to it that requires a deeper outlook before proper implementation, considering you have a plan that is passing through stages of the DEI Lighthouse Framework. There has to be adequate context to the idea as you proceed, and it starts with offering clarity to what employment equity signifies.

The Fourth DEI Lighthouse Framework emphasizes the importance of actively designing solutions that will stand the test of time. Organizations need to move beyond superficial diversity efforts and work on structural changes, and this involves ensuring that all employees, regardless of their background, have equal opportunities to thrive within the organization. As a leader, rethink recruitment, promotions, and workplace culture. Ask questions about what's going wrong with the system and seek opinions to help mitigate whatever is hampering the smooth sail of DEI, and while you're at it, be sure you truly understand all about employment equity.

When it comes to employment equity, you must look at it beyond being discrimination but, as a tool to address systemic imbalances. Cases where some groups have historically faced more barriers than others in terms of access to career growth, possibly because of their color, personality, orientation, and more. You might have been forced to make tough choices because you didn't get the kind of opportunities others received. Such disparities are why these initiatives aim to level the playing field and provide everyone with a fair shot at success.

But first, as you strive to engage any plan, recognize that it's vital to distinguish between employment equity and discrimination. Employment equity is the antithesis of discrimination because while it promotes fairness and equal opportunities, discrimination perpetuates inequities and awakens an awareness of color, religion, status, and more. Once you can differentiate both adequately, you will give sound advocacy for more equitable plans that involve a proactive approach to fostering inclusion. A plan that goes beyond paperwork but reveals an honest approach with genuine commitment and implementation to take actionable steps from the organization's leadership to the employees concerned.

You need to see it to believe it. That's what implementation involves, beginning with creating a culture where everyone feels valued and has an equal chance to contribute their best. Collective ongoing effort within the organization becomes part and parcel of the mission and vision until it runs deep in the company's DNA. Achieving the implementation process which can be done by Human Resources or senior executives takes convincing employees of the benefits of having and building an equitable system for the now and the future.

Benefits of Equity

- **Safe Environment:** The enormous safety employees attain knowing their promotion and their background or identity does not determine career advancement is the first step to making a successful entry for implementing employment equity. You put your best foot forward to work because you feel valued and accepted without judgment.
- **Promoting Innovation and Creativity:** When people from different cultures and orientations come together to work and share ideas, there is a quality of work that comes out of that combination that is exceptional because it's a source

beyond a regular path. Like a meal with different ingredients and spices, this is a mix that spurs outstanding innovations and inclusivity.

- **Enabling Opportunity for Youths:** Young people, as well as minorities, with the help of employment equity, begin to see the opportunities that exist for everyone, regardless of their background. Suppose they believed their passion for success was a pipe dream because of the issue of discrimination. In that case, it gets dispelled as the representation of employment equity is critical in inspiring and empowering underrepresented groups to pursue their aspirations and be rest assured of having equal opportunities.

- **Increases Trust and Collaboration:** If there is one thing a diverse workforce attracts with the right framework for equity, it is trust among employees. Once they see that their organization values and respects differences, the trust enhances collaboration because employees, as diverse teams as they have become, now have a deeper understanding of each other, leading to improved teamwork and problem-solving.

- **Better Retention Plan:** DEI principles create a sense of belonging for employees from underrepresented communities. It is vital to attract, retain, and promote diverse talent in the system. Employees who see your commitment to their satisfaction and consistent loyalty through adequate equity will give them all to ensure the organization moves to greater heights. That way, growth and progress are all around.

- **Uniquely Tailored Plan:** Every organization's employment equity plan is tailored to specific needs and circumstances. There is no one-size-fits-all solution, and companies must design strategies that align with their goals, culture, and existing diversity landscape as it spurs creativity. Based on the brand, an approach could work better for one and not the other. Google and Gucci can never have similar employment equity plans. Although these brands aim to serve the public, they represent two industries and focus on different missions and visions.

- **Tracking, Monitoring, and Revision:** Employment equity requires ongoing monitoring and revision to make it count. Data-driven assessments help organizations identify areas that need improvement, allowing them to adjust their strategies for more effective equity initiatives. No need to fret if the figures don't look great because they fluctuate depending on time, trends, and feedback as the implementation progresses.

As time elapses, the benefits of equity in employment show itself as a non-negotiable necessity that all leaders embrace and aim for to make employees hunger to be part of any workspace. All HR and executives must take extra steps in fashioning out ways to make a success out of convincing employees that their unique skills, talents, and achievements aren't only appreciated but are valued and respected.

The goal is to be open to every possibility by:

1. **Creating Room:** Create an inclusive environment that accommodates various health conditions and disabilities, whether the blind, autistic, or aged. Knowing blind people might require braille to enable their reading or hard-of-hearing individuals some form of hearing aid, make all necessary adjustments to the workspace. You can have assistive technologies and offer flexible work arrangements to ensure all employees perform at their best. Nothing should make employees feel depressed to executive their jobs and feel as involved as everyone else.

2. **Wage Equity:** Pay equity is a fundamental aspect of DEI, and when there is a regular review and adjustment to wages, employees are compensated fairly based on their skills,

experience, and job responsibilities. No favoritism but an address to any wage gaps that may exist among different demographic groups.

3. **Wage Transparency:** Promote wage transparency in your organization. Ensure that employees understand the criteria used for determining their compensation. Transparent pay structures align with the principle of equal pay for equal work and play a crucial role in addressing historical pay disparities based on gender, race, or age. By making salary information accessible, organizations build trust among their workforce, boosting morale and employee confidence in the fairness of the compensation system. Also, with it, you can motivate employees to enhance their performance and skills, knowing how their pay is determined. Additionally, it ensures compliance with legal requirements related to pay gaps and contributes to attracting a diverse and inclusive talent pool. Ultimately, wage transparency is a powerful tool for promoting fairness, reducing bias, and fostering a workplace environment where every individual's contributions are recognized and compensated justly.

4. **Equity Awareness Structure:** You can create a workplace culture that values equity and shows it by educating employees about the importance of equity and inclusion. Open dialogues about equity-related issues, workshops, and providing resources to help employees understand their rights and responsibilities will raise a continual assessment of the effectiveness of all things equity, from awareness to initiatives. So, along with these programs, you regularly monitor and evaluate workplace equity through surveys, feedback mechanisms, and key performance indicators. The data becomes useful for making data-driven decisions about the right awareness initiative and so much more to identify areas for improvement.

5. **Equity Goals:** Transparency in setting and sharing equity goals demonstrates a commitment to a fair and inclusive

workplace. You can have clear and shared goals, thereby becoming a rallying point for all employees so everyone has a sense of shared responsibility. It encourages everyone to contribute to these objectives, and with regular assessment and adaptation, the organization will learn and grow in its equity journey.

6. **Team Empowerment:** Diverse teams are not just about optics; they're dynamic engines for creativity and innovation. My perspective emphasizes that when you prioritize diverse leadership and encourage varied voices at all levels, you invite a range of perspectives that can lead to novel solutions. This diversity isn't just a checkbox but a catalyst for staying competitive in a rapidly evolving global landscape.

7. **Reforming Hiring Practices:** Rethinking hiring practices to reflect equitable policies isn't just about compliance but fundamental fairness. It's a shift that allows you to showcase your organization's commitment to merit-based hiring. By focusing on skills and qualifications, you ensure that candidates are selected based on their ability to excel in their roles, creating a more capable and diverse workforce.

8. **Involving Online Presence:** Your website is often the first interaction potential employees have with your organization. As a leader, use it to highlight your diversity and inclusion initiatives. It communicates that your workplace is not just a collection of employees striving for company success but a vibrant community where diversity is celebrated. This makes your organization attractive to candidates who value equity.

9. **Inclusive Onboarding:** Onboarding goes beyond the logistical processes; it's the first exposure a new employee has to your workplace culture. So when you want to entice a new hire by convincing them through an inclusive onboarding process, it sends a clear message that your organization values every individual's unique skills and talents and is eager to create an environment where all employees can thrive, irrespective of their background.

Activities to Promote Equity in the Workplace

To promote equity and encourage acceptance, understanding, and implementation of diversity and inclusion in the workplace, engaging activities can be organized. As a leader and an executive, you can spring up the best ideas to spur DEI in the workplace and surprise your employees.

Activity 1: Virtual Travels Details

Virtual travels can be enhanced by dedicating specific sessions to regions or countries with unique workplace cultures. Include guided discussions after each session to reflect on how these cultural insights can be applied to build an inclusive work environment. All you have to do is encourage team members to share personal experiences related to the featured culture, reinforcing the importance of understanding and appreciating diversity.

Activity 2: Spot the Brand to Support Details

This activity can go beyond brand recognition. Organize follow-up sessions where team members share their experiences with products from diverse brands. Discuss how supporting these brands positively impacts the economy and the employment of underrepresented groups. Go above and beyond by inviting entrepreneurs from these brands to share their journeys, providing a deeper understanding of the challenges they face, and making employees understand that: "Hey it's not as bad as people make it out to be."

Activity 3: Real-Life Storytelling Details

To make real-life storytelling more impactful, encourage participants to highlight moments of growth and transformation regarding their perceptions of diversity and inclusion. These stories can serve as catalysts for organizational change, inspiring others to rethink their perspectives and biases, whether right or wrong, while considering having a trained facilitator to ensure these conversations remain respectful, constructive, and valuable to all parties.

Activity 4: Differences Aside Details

Provide resources such as articles, books, or documentaries in advance that focus on various aspects of DEI. Encourage participants to engage with these materials and come prepared to discuss their key takeaways. Create a welcoming environment where participants can ask questions and seek clarification about issues they may not fully understand or turn it into a game where somehow fun is created so the topic doesn't seem uptight or create a kind of nervous tension.

Activity 5: Office Potluck Details

To add depth to the office potluck, encourage participants to bring food and share stories or traditions related to the dishes they bring. Imagine the fun of having a variety of foods brought to the table; it spices up the networking occasion. This personal touch helps team members connect on a deeper level and appreciate the cultural significance of the food. Consider incorporating a rotation system so each team member can host a potluck and share their heritage. Such an organization will be the envy of many growing companies once they observe and notice the exchange of respect, harmony, and connection employees have with each other and their employers. The environment will ooze with DEI as an achievement and a way of life.

Clearly, it shows that your differences don't define you. Instead, they might be your Pandora's box. So, embrace them, welcome the changes at work, or incorporate your plan as a leader. At the same time the focus remains, as always, on establishing ways of bringing inclusion to the workplace.

7

BOLD INCLUSION—THE BEGINNING OF VALUE, RESPECT, AND PRICELESS TEAMWORK

Diversity is a mix, and inclusion is making the mix work.
—Andres Tapia (Teambuilding, 2022)

Climbing the Fourth Step

By now, you already know that diversity and inclusion are what make the workplace a place to thrive. Glassdoor (2021) reveals that among job candidates, roughly two-thirds, or roughly 67%, express a strong preference for organizations that boast a diverse workforce. This preference highlights the growing importance of workplace diversity in the eyes of potential employees.

Furthermore, a striking 74% of millennial employees firmly believe that their respective organizations demonstrate greater levels of innovation when they cultivate a culture of inclusion. This sentiment underscores the critical link between diversity and innovation, emphasizing that companies embracing a wide range of perspectives tend to excel in innovative thinking. Intriguingly, almost half of millennials, specifically 47%, actively factor in a company's commitment to diversity and inclusion when evaluating potential employers.

This statistic illustrates that a significant portion of the workforce, particularly the millennial generation, is making a conscious effort to align their career choices with organizations that share their values and prioritize diversity and inclusion (Deloitte, 2023).

There is no other way to say it: DEI is the future of successful workplaces, and now that we are at the fourth step of the Lighthouse Framework, the final stage to make a difference. It is time to uncover the contexts that reveal practical daily changes that can be achieved using DEI starting with defining inclusion from a more personable perspective.

Inclusion extends beyond just creating a sense of belonging at work. It involves nurturing an environment where diversity isn't just tolerated but celebrated. When it comes to inclusive organizations, it's about actively investing in policies and practices that ensure people from all backgrounds feel respected, valued, and empowered to contribute their unique talents. Such environments foster innovation, as people are more likely to share diverse perspectives, resulting in creative problem-solving metrics because no one's ideas are shut down. Now, there are several ways in which an inclusive organization can sustain its vision permanently:

- **Ground Up:** Building inclusion from the ground up is the way to go, where individuals at all levels of an organization play important roles in driving change beyond the responsibility of senior management. Frontline employees, middle managers, and executives, all with their unique perspectives and power, make a workplace more inclusive through collaboration; a multi-level approach is often more effective than top-down strategies.
- **Integration of Inclusive Practices:** In all daily routines, inclusive practices should become second nature beyond policy documents and training sessions. This means inclusivity becomes a part of the cultural DNA of the

organization, ingrained in the day-to-day activities, thereby making it more likely to be sustained.

- **Voice for All:** Giving every individual a voice doesn't just mean providing a platform for speaking out; it's about actively listening, valuing, and acting on those voices. Inclusive organizations not only encourage feedback but also demonstrate that they take it seriously, leading to greater engagement and trust among employees.
- **Uniqueness and Belonging:** Acknowledging uniqueness and fostering belonging requires a proactive approach to valuing differences, such as background, experiences, and perspectives. They make sure every employee feels that their distinct qualities contribute to the organization's success, fostering a deep sense of belonging.
- **Consistent Recognition:** Recognizing and celebrating the uniqueness of each employee is not a one-time event. Inclusive organizations continually affirm the value of diversity. This recognition isn't just about big gestures; it can happen through daily interactions, feedback, and acknowledgment of contributions, no matter how small.
- **Learning and Development:** In an inclusive environment, learning and development are tailored to individual needs and aspirations. It's not just about generic training; it's about providing opportunities for growth that are relevant and meaningful to each employee, ensuring their potential is fully realized.
- **Collaboration:** This is about teamwork, diversity of thought, and harnessing the power of varied perspectives to drive innovation and solve complex challenges. Collaborative efforts are highly valued and encouraged, driving productivity and creativity.
- **Resource Accessibility:** Ensuring employees have access to necessary resources means addressing potential barriers, whether physical, technological, or cultural. An inclusive

workplace actively seeks to remove these barriers to create an environment where all can thrive.

- **Intrinsic Motivation:** Cultivate a culture where employees feel intrinsically motivated to contribute tirelessly to the growth of an organization. They are aligned with the organization's mission and values, which, in turn, fosters a strong sense of belonging and engagement.

- **Transparency and Support:** Transparency extends to sharing information about the organization's DEI initiatives and progress. Support means not only offering resources but also introducing a culture where employees feel comfortable seeking assistance and mentorship, leading to personal and professional growth.

No doubt, with all these in place, Inclusion benefits organizations by improving employee morale, driving creativity and innovation, and increasing productivity. For workers, it offers the opportunity to work in an environment where they can thrive and achieve their potential, contributing to a more fulfilling and successful career.

Steps to Imbibe Inclusion in the Workplace

Above all, knowing the potential inclusion brings to the table makes it paramount for individuals to seek ways to imbibe the rule of inclusion as a character in the workplace. It starts by taking these steps:

- **Embrace Your Authenticity in the Workplace:** Being authentic in the workplace not only fosters a more inclusive environment but also enhances your well-being. When you are genuine, you're more likely to connect with your colleagues on a personal level, which can lead to better teamwork and collaboration. Make yourself felt and understood through your ideas, and your team members will see you as a colleague who represents authenticity.

- **Practice Thoughtful Communication:** Thoughtful communication is a cornerstone of effective workplace interactions. It not only helps prevent misunderstandings but also promotes a culture of respect and consideration. Taking a moment to reflect on your words can save you from unintentional offense and help you convey your thoughts more clearly. When you send a message in a group chat, be mindful of your tone and diction as well as the emojis used so you don't create doubt as to your character due to statements made casually.
- **Connect Through Personal Experiences:** Sharing your own experiences can be a powerful tool for building empathy and understanding among your colleagues. It helps humanize the workplace, making it easier for others to relate to you and your perspectives, which in turn encourages a more inclusive atmosphere.
- **Respect by Using Correct Pronouns:** Using correct pronouns is a sign of respect for your colleagues' identities. It not only ensures that they feel acknowledged and valued but also sets an example for others, creating an inclusive space for everyone.
- **Champion Diversity and Differences:** Celebrating diversity in the workplace isn't just the right thing to do; it's also a source of strength. Differences in perspectives, backgrounds, and experiences can lead to more innovative solutions and richer collaboration. Supporting these differences contributes to a more vibrant and inclusive work environment.
- **Stay Informed About Inclusive Language:** Language and terminology evolve, and keeping up with these changes is a sign of being respectful and inclusive. Your willingness to educate yourself and adapt your language demonstrates your commitment to fostering a diverse and welcoming workspace.

- **Enhance Clarity with Universal Phrases:** Using universal phrases in communication helps ensure that everyone is on the same page. It minimizes misunderstandings and ensures that your message is accessible to all, regardless of their background or knowledge.
- **Respect Nonbinary Identities with Gender-Neutral Language:** Genderless language is a simple yet impactful way to be inclusive of nonbinary individuals. It sends a powerful message that you acknowledge and respect diverse gender identities, contributing to a more inclusive workplace.
- **Foster Understanding Through Thoughtful Questions:** Showing thoughtfulness and a willingness to learn by seeking clarification when faced with unfamiliar concepts or terms fosters an environment where asking questions is encouraged. This can lead to richer discussions and a deeper understanding of each other's perspectives.
- **Educate Yourself About Colleagues' Experiences:** Commit to educating yourself about others' experiences and challenges, recognizing the value of your example in fostering inclusion. Life is much more than just about us; it's about the people around us and how their experiences can shape our reality. So, never make anything in life about just you, especially when you are part of an inclusive workforce.
- **Show Respect Through Active Listening:** Active listening is fundamental to respectful and inclusive communication. When you don't interrupt, you signal that you value your colleagues' input and respect their expertise. This can lead to more meaningful and constructive interactions.
- **Recognize and Appreciate Contributions:** Acknowledging and appreciating individual contributions is a form of recognition that can boost morale and motivation. Redirecting questions to the right experts shows respect for their expertise and ensures that individuals are recognized for their specific contributions.

- **Provide Constructive Feedback Without Personal Attacks:** Feedback that focuses on situations rather than personal attacks encourages a culture of respect, open communication, and continuous improvement. It fosters an environment where everyone feels safe to share ideas and make mistakes without fear of personal criticism.
- **Actively Interrupt Microaggressions:** Interrupting microaggressions is not only an act of allyship but also a way to actively contribute to a safe, inclusive environment by sending messages that such behaviors are not tolerated. It encourages others to follow suit and support colleagues who may be experiencing microaggressions. You can use examples to buttress practicing microaggression interruptions and help build the skills needed to address these issues effectively. It's a proactive step toward creating a more inclusive and respectful workplace.

Once the employees have successfully accomplished their part in practice, it doesn't end there. HR, leaders, and executives must fulfill their end of the bargain by finding easy and accommodating ways to invite inclusion into the workplace.

1. **Prioritize Inclusive Policies:** Begin by ensuring that your organization has comprehensive, up-to-date, inclusive policies in place. These policies should cover various aspects of diversity, equity, and inclusion, including hiring practices, employee development, and cultural awareness training. Building a culture of inclusion often requires buy-in and active support from leadership and HR teams.
2. **Lead by Revealing Pronouns:** Demonstrate your commitment to inclusivity by disclosing your pronouns. Encourage all team members to follow suit, creating an environment where everyone can express their gender identity comfortably. Providing this visibility is particularly

vital for transgender and nonbinary individuals, offering a welcoming and respectful atmosphere.

3. **Incorporate Cultural Celebrations and Observances:** Show genuine appreciation for the diverse backgrounds and traditions of your employees and colleagues by incorporating a range of cultural celebrations and observances into the company calendar. This sends a clear message that the organization values and respects the varied cultural heritages of its workforce.

4. **Establish Safe and Inclusive Spaces:** Proactively create safe and inclusive spaces within the workplace, including facilities for nursing mothers, prayer rooms, or quiet spaces for meditation. These efforts ensure that employees from all backgrounds feel respected and accommodated.

5. **Foster Inclusivity Through Team-Building Events:** Planning and participating in inclusive team-building events is an excellent way to encourage connections among employees from diverse backgrounds. As a leader, consider the types of activities and events that will be inclusive and supportive, ensuring everyone feels a sense of belonging.

6. **Recognize and Reward Equitably:** Guarantee that recognition and rewards are distributed fairly. Implement a system that acknowledges and values the contributions of all employees, regardless of their background, tenure, or level of achievement. This practice motivates and engages all team members, fostering a sense of belonging.

7. **Accessibility for All Employees:** As HR, an executive, and a leader, it's imperative to ensure that the workplace is accessible to all employees. This includes accommodating remote workers, individuals with disabilities, and those with different accessibility needs. Embracing accessibility fosters an inclusive and supportive environment where all can thrive.

8. **Adopt Inclusive Language Year-Round:** Demonstrate an unwavering commitment to respect and inclusivity by

consistently using inclusive language throughout the year. Avoiding offensive language or terminology fosters a culture of understanding and acceptance.

9. **Join Inclusion Allies Programs:** Participate in inclusion allies programs to deepen your understanding of diversity and inclusion issues. These programs provide valuable insights and equip you to support employees from underrepresented backgrounds actively. By actively engaging in these programs, you become a champion of inclusivity.

10. **Display Multilingual Signage and Materials:** Reinforce the message of welcome and inclusivity by installing multilingual signage and providing materials in various languages. These materials also serve as gentle reminders to employees that they are part of a diverse, global community, regardless of the language spoken in the office.

All these approaches don't work in isolation; there has to be a regularity of events where there is prompting the question of how can you assemble a team that not only values inclusivity but also forms strong bonds, enhancing their ability to collaborate innovatively and creatively. Doing this often will inform everyone that anyone is welcome to propose activities to introduce what can be called a tighter-knit and more innovative team. You can test with activities.

Activity 1: The Chat Away

The focus is on open and candid discussions within the workplace. Drawing inspiration from the talk show format of Steve Harvey and Ellen DeGeneres, this initiative aims to create a platform where employees feel encouraged to share their experiences and perspectives openly. The goal is to establish a space for honest inclusivity, allowing diverse voices to be heard and valued. Much like the talk show hosts, the objective is to generate meaningful dialogues around various social issues, so the work environment becomes that place where lessons are learned, and innovative ideas are embraced.

Instructions

- Encourage employees to openly share their experiences and perspectives.
- Create a platform where diverse voices are welcomed and valued.
- Take inspiration from talk shows like Steve Harvey and Ellen DeGeneres, where candid conversations are celebrated.
- Feature guests from diverse backgrounds, promoting inclusivity and understanding.
- Embrace the emotions that may arise during discussions, with the understanding that lessons learned contribute to personal and collective growth.
- Ensure that the chat-away moments lead to a workplace culture where inclusivity holds significance.

Activity 2: Picture Albums

Create team picture albums to celebrate the diversity within the organization. These albums will visually capture the unique backgrounds, cultural experiences, and encounters of team members through vibrant colors, collages, and canvas.

Instructions

- Gather photos that represent the diverse backgrounds, cultural travels, and experiences of team members.
- Design visually appealing collages that showcase the richness of cultural diversity within the team.
- Experiment with different artistic mediums, such as canvas, to add a touch of creativity to the picture albums.
- Take inspiration from the "Share a Coke" campaign by Coca-Cola, emphasizing personalization and representation of various cultural backgrounds.
- Use the picture albums as a means to promote inclusivity and connection within the team.

- Aim for the lasting impact achieved by campaigns like "Share a Coke" by making the picture albums a symbol of cohesion and celebration of diversity.

Activity 3: A Thousand Words

Embrace the timeless tradition of storytelling infused with modern creativity. This activity encourages employees to share their stories through visual elements, combining the richness of personal experiences with creative images.

Instructions

- Invite employees to share personal stories emphasizing unique perspectives and experiences.
- Emphasize using creative images, graphics, or visual elements to enhance the storytelling experience.
- Compile the visual stories into a showcase or gallery, either virtually or physically, celebrating individual uniqueness.
- Encourage continuous participation, creating a dynamic and evolving tapestry of employee experiences.

Activity 4: Privilege and Allyship

This activity explores privilege and allyship. It educates employees on the concept of privilege and encourages them to be allies for their colleagues. If an employee has faced some form of abuse in her past, of course, she wouldn't know what it's like to feel supported and loved by a partner because she never had it. However, it doesn't mean she needs to feel alien to a discussion that surrounds either side of the coin as regards love and abuse. For such an individual, they must be carried along to understand the privileges of support and also appreciate that they aren't alone but have allies they can trust to stand by them. It builds understanding and support among employees so that there is a space for open dialogue. Here, no one feels alienated from discussions on various life experiences.

Instructions

- Conduct a session explaining the concept of privilege, using examples to help employees grasp its nuances.
- Prompt employees to reflect on their own experiences and acknowledge areas where privilege plays a role.
- Facilitate discussions on the importance of allyship, emphasizing the role each employee can play in supporting their colleagues.
- Relate the concept to real-world examples, such as the advocacy initiatives of companies like Ben & Jerry's, illustrating the power of allyship in driving positive change.

Activity 5: The Name Game

This activity centers on fostering a workplace culture that respects individuals' names and pronouns. It emphasizes the significance of using correct terms to create an inclusive environment.

Instructions

- Begin with a brief educational session on the importance of using correct names and pronouns, drawing attention to the evolving landscape of gender identification.
- Reference notable figures like Laverne Cox, who advocates for transgender rights and emphasizes the impact of using correct pronouns.
- Encourage an open dialogue where employees can share their preferred pronouns, fostering an understanding of diverse gender identities within the team.
- Ensure workplace materials and platforms incorporate spaces for individuals to specify their preferred pronouns, promoting visibility and respect.
- Implement periodic reminders and updates on the importance of using correct names and pronouns to reinforce a culture of inclusivity.

Note: Sensitivity and respect are paramount during this activity to create a safe space for open discussion.

Activity 6: Inclusive Design Workshops

Organizing workshops where employees collaborate to design products, services, or workplace elements with inclusivity in mind is another activity that might seem casual but can be most rewarding of all. This promotes a more equitable and innovative environment. For instance, in a technology company, the HR department wanted to make their workplace more accessible for employees with disabilities. They organized an inclusive design workshop, bringing together employees from various departments and an inclusive design expert. The workshop focused on identifying challenges, brainstorming solutions, and creating prototypes for inclusive design changes. These changes, such as accessible ramps and sensory-friendly workspaces, were then implemented! Think of the amount of inclusivity that will be created for the disabled group and how valued they will feel knowing their participation is desired and appreciated.

How about this setting:

Instructions

- Clearly define the objective of making the workplace more accessible for employees with disabilities.
- Assemble a diverse group, including employees from various departments and an inclusive design expert.
- Break the workshop into phases—identify challenges, brainstorm solutions, and create prototypes for inclusive design changes.
- Ensure the inclusive design expert guides participants, providing insights into best practices.
- Select and implement feasible solutions, such as accessible ramps and sensory-friendly workspaces.
- Communicate changes to the workforce, emphasizing collective effort, and celebrate the success of the workshop.

So, with these activities incorporated into the workplace, organizations can be sure to head on to foster inclusivity and innovation. These are activities that provide opportunities for employees to learn from each other's diverse experiences, creating a culture that values differences and encourages creativity. With the insights and strategies provided in the previous sections, you'll be well-equipped to assemble a comprehensive and confident plan. The final two strategies delve into the critical aspects of modeling best practices, leading by example, and effectively addressing any potential challenges that may surface during your DEI integration. Notably, the solutions you develop for these challenges will further enhance the overall effectiveness of your DEI plan, as discussed in Chapter Three. Now, let's shift our focus to your role in this transformative journey.

8

THE PRIZE OF MULTICULTURAL WORKPLACES

Earn your leadership every day.
—*Michael Jordan (Sankofa, 2023)*

You

In the scheme of DEI, there is one thing that completes the meal: you. If you didn't know, understand that the prize for making a multicultural workplace is all about how you commit yourself to this needed change in the workplace. In case you missed it, you hold the four aces; you represent the 92% of leaders and executives who believe training and workshops presented by passionate DEI drivers are the prize of gaining a multicultural workplace (Instride, 2020).

You are guided to delve deep into your DEI mindset and become the driving force behind the change you want to see. You are not only a participant but a mentor, inspiring and leading by example to ignite DEI progress. You might be curious why you have become the protagonist in this 8th strategy. It's because you're the one with the idea; therefore, the realms of change demand more from you.

- **A Deep Commitment and Accountability:** Within the DEI Lighthouse Model, a profound commitment is essential. This means being responsible for the changes, investing in them, and actively modeling the desired transformations within the organization.
- **Being the Epicenter of Change:** As a leader, you are the focal point for all transformative efforts. To initiate and sustain progress, embrace diversity, consistently monitor key metrics, seek feedback, and acknowledge and reward those who contribute to the change journey.
- **Kickstarting with Role Model Leadership:** To inspire others to follow your lead in championing diversity and inclusion, actively engage in the process, and display the qualities of a role model leader. Effective role models can overcome obstacles and serve as beacons of positive change.
- **Involvement and Role Modeling:** To drive the transformation you envision, it's crucial to be as involved as you expect others to be. By taking the lead and actively participating, you become a role model for the changes you aspire to instill within the organization. This involves demonstrating the qualities that others should emulate.

Note that effective role model leaders exhibit qualities that make them worthy of emulation. These qualities include resilience, determination, adaptability, empathy, and the ability to inspire and guide others.

Ways to Exhibit Role Model Persona

So what are the ways you can exhibit the role model persona so others follow accordingly and you, in turn, see the right DEI results?

1. **The Hard Work Foundation:** No one likes to be overworked or work so hard it takes away their fun time or makes them lose their sense of concern for other things in life. But, when you really work hard with a goal, it forms the cornerstone of

effective role modeling. You stay dedicated to tasks and maintain a mentality where excuses aren't tolerated or entertained because you know once you begin to think of all the reasons why it can't or won't work, a lot of people will be disappointed, considering how much confidence they have in you. Probably more than you did in yourself. Consider the determination and diligence displayed by Oprah Winfrey, who overcame significant obstacles to achieve success in media. She was committed because she understood that this wasn't just about her, or women in the media or women in the workplace, but women of color who needed to feel safe anywhere in the world, and that's why Oprah serves as an inspiration for all today.

2. **The Trust Mechanism:** This is an element of being a role model that helps more people buy into your idea and participate in your cause. You should prove to your team that you can be trusted by consistently exhibiting fairness in judgments, honesty in dealings, and reliability in moments of struggle. If there is office gossip going on because of a manager who messed up or an executive whose integrity is in question, don't be the one to spread the already bad news and discourage it within your team. As a leader, building trust among employees gives them the assurance that their issues are in the hands of someone who takes confidentiality seriously.

3. **Accountability Mode:** If you're afraid to be blamed when things go wrong, especially when you represent the center of a project, then ask yourself if you really want to be a role model. In this position, you must learn to take responsibility for your actions so you inspire others to do the same. In cases of mistakes or missteps, admit them and communicate your plan for correction because roles come with failures and successes, and you need to have a taste of both, so you appreciate what it means to develop. Leadership accountability assists organizations in preparing for seasons

when a business experiences downsides and economic loopholes occur, at such times all hands must come together to ensure transparency for survival. This was one of the measures that made people appreciate Elon Musk's accountability mode during challenging times at SpaceX, where he showcased the importance of taking responsibility and addressing issues directly.

4. **Respect Response:** The respect response is paramount in all interactions role models have and will have going forward between themselves, employees, and stakeholders. Showing respect to individuals, whether they are customers, employees, or vendors, proves you understand the importance of value and that every individual has self-worth in your eyes. It's especially vital when addressing behavioral issues, which often pop up in workplaces when intentions and statements are misinterpreted or misconstrued. When Indra Nooyi, the former CEO of PepsiCo, exemplified respect by promoting a culture of inclusivity and respect for diverse perspectives within her company, she did it with the intent to uphold DEI as a business imperative. Indra sustained that if you want to get the most suited hands at work in any business, it starts with the entire population. If you comb through a larger number, there is no telling the amount of talent and skill you will find hungry to give their all (Peterson, 2020).

5. **Optimistic Positivity:** Maintaining a positive outlook during times of change is essential.There is such a thing as toxic positivity, where you stand confident and reassured in your mind that no matter the challenges that come, everything is going to be alright, and you maintain keeping the workplace that way because, for you, optimistic positivity is the anchor for DEI.

6. **Demonstrating Integrity:** As a role model, you must adhere to the same rules you expect your team to follow. Never exempt yourself from being subject to the rules just because

you are a leader and executive. If employees don't see you uphold the existence of DEI as a necessity, what should they do? Howard Schultz, the former CEO of Starbucks, has shown remarkable integrity throughout his career by consistently following company policies and setting an example of integrity. He projected a culture of trust and ethics within Starbucks. He looked at how renowned the business is and how it maintains its status despite the challenges of COVID-19 and many other economic meltdowns.

7. **Persistence Metrics:** Role models display steady persistence in the face of obstacles. Whether you're at the entry level or a seasoned professional, becoming a role model in your workplace starts with showcasing qualities that others can look up to. Microsoft's CEO, Satya Nadella, made a difference when he championed DEI in the tech industry by implementing programs for equal opportunities and employee support, a commitment that set high standards for the industry.

As you become more visible in your role as a leader, mentor, or someone actively embodying the principles you want to instill in others, the time comes to shift from personal change to inspiring those around you. Whether you're striving to make (DEI) stand out or other transformative values, leading by example is paramount. It involves showcasing your drive for DEI through your actions and communication. Sharing your own DEI journey, complete with its trials and triumphs, can inspire others, create an atmosphere where every voice is heard and respected, and welcome open dialogues and active listening. When experience can be told in stories recounting real-life tales of individuals who've overcome DEI challenges, serves as an impactful source of motivation. Recognizing and celebrating even small DEI victories reinforces your dedication. As a mentor or leader, you play a proactive role in nurturing personal growth, providing educational opportunities, and setting ambitious yet achievable goals. With your ability to inspire, you can lead your organization toward a future of positive transformation and innovation in several ways unimaginable:

- Set high goals aligning with your chapter three plan, and aim for them, no matter what, to prove your ambition for success and how goals are an essential part of your plan. These goals should be in tune with your strategic DEI plan, and once there is a continuous striving to achieve these goals, you lead by example and inspire your colleagues to be equally dedicated to the cause.
- Use empathy to show how much you care about other cultures and minorities in your journey as a DEI advocate. When you can trigger the right kind of emotion in people using shared personal stories of cultural experiences or moments of inclusivity, it can go a long way in demonstrating genuine care for other cultures and minorities. As a leader, you dig deep into what makes a person thick and ensure they know how valued they are; by extension, others will accord the employee the same level of care, respect, and value, and possibly more.
- Show interest and appreciation for things they achieve at home or work by celebrating them in any way possible. A significant aspect of inspiring others is recognizing and appreciating their achievements, both in their personal lives and at work. As you actively root for them and acknowledge their successes, you create a culture of support and inclusivity where every individual's contributions are put out there, not as a show-off but as a show of support.
- Practice good communication, inclusive language, active listening, and knowing the pronouns colleagues prefer. By consistently using inclusive language, actively listening to your colleagues, and respecting their preferred pronouns, you set a clear example of respectful and inclusive

communication. This practice empowers your team to do the same.

- Empowering your colleagues by suggesting and creating shared opportunities is a hallmark of inspirational leadership. It shows that you are committed to their growth and development. I've witnessed firsthand how these opportunities can bring diverse talents to the forefront.

- Share the personal and professional benefits of DEI, and speak plainly about the insights with your colleagues. When the positive impact it has had on your own journey is stated, many will want to engage with DEI initiatives and embrace its rewards actively.

- Using storytelling to inspire others to speak up and share their own experiences and challenges related to diversity and inclusion, along with your personal growth, can encourage them to open up and celebrate their own differences. I've found that storytelling creates an emotional connection that motivates others to share and embrace their unique narratives.

- Demonstrating a genuine interest in learning about your colleagues is a cornerstone of encouraging inclusivity. By investing time in understanding their backgrounds, experiences, and interests, you show that you value their uniqueness. This, in turn, creates a sense of belonging and trust within the team.

- In meetings or casual conversations, asking the right questions is an effective way to inspire others. Thought-provoking questions encourage meaningful dialogue, critical thinking, and the sharing of diverse perspectives. I've observed how this practice promotes a culture of open and inclusive communication.

- Building intentional relationships with colleagues from diverse backgrounds is a personal commitment every role model must hold dire. It's a conscious effort to connect with individuals, regardless of their cultural origins. This approach not only strengthens professional bonds but also sets a powerful example of building an inclusive workplace.

All the personal growth mechanism shared takes us to the realm of effective communication, as this is an action often conveying more than words alone. Nevertheless, mastering the art of combining body language, speech, and tone can significantly impact your ability to influence and connect with your colleagues. Let's delve into strategies for enhancing your communication in a professional setting.

Strategies to Enhance Communication

Active Listening Skills

In this setting, you should be able to:

- Maintaining **eye contact** demonstrates your engagement and respect for the speaker, thereby building trust and rapport. You're sending the message that you value what they have to say and that they have your full attention.
- People often communicate as much through their body language, facial expressions, and tone as they do with words. By paying **attention to these cues**, you can gain a deeper understanding of the speaker's emotions and perspectives. For instance, a coworker may say they're fine, but their slouched posture and averted gaze might suggest otherwise.
- Interrupting can be perceived as disrespectful and may hinder open dialogue. **Allowing the speaker to finish** their thoughts shows that you respect their perspective and are willing to listen before forming your response.
- When you listen without judgment, you create a safe space for honest and open communication. **Avoiding hasty judgments** allows the speaker to express themselves freely without fear of criticism.

- Instead of immediately providing your own opinions or solutions, focus on **understanding the speaker's viewpoint.** Your goal is not to fix the issue but to grasp their perspective fully.
- **Asking questions** not only demonstrates your interest but also helps clarify and deepen your understanding. It's a way to show that you're actively engaged in the conversation.

Effective Communication

With active listening comes a more detailed idea of how communication is made impactful from role models to employees:

- **Authenticity** is essential in building trust. Being yourself in your communication is more genuine and the best in a transparent environment where colleagues can relate to you more readily, seeing how much of a realist you are.
- In a professional setting, **clear and transparent communication** is vital. Transparency in your messages ensures that others can comprehend your intentions and expectations without confusion. Nothing is misread or misunderstood because you made it so.
- **Simplifying your communication** is crucial, especially in the workplace. Avoid jargon or overly complex language that might confuse others. Being direct ensures that your message is clear and easily understood. Sometimes, in a bid to sound professional, we add too much to straightforward ideas, and in the end, nothing is established. You have to be intentional about being understood.
- **Storytelling** is a powerful communication tool. Sharing relevant stories or anecdotes can make your points more relatable, memorable, and engaging. It helps convey complex ideas in a way that's easy to grasp and can bring about valid emotional responses.

- **Non-verbal elements** can reinforce your message. Gestures, body language, and tone can emphasize your sincerity and intent, contributing to a more comprehensive understanding of your communication. The way you laugh when employees make an error will determine if the laugh is out of anger, mockery, or a way to lighten the mood so they don't feel like an error is a death sentence.

- **Receiving feedback** gracefully and acting upon it demonstrates your willingness to improve and adapt. It's a sign of a growth-oriented, learning mindset and also that you are willing to take the fall for any error so that you can make things right.

- The most compelling form of communication is your **actions.** Following through on your commitments, demonstrating consistency, and acting on your words build trust and credibility in your workplace relationships.

Actionable Steps

Having considered all these, what about actionable steps that can lay the foundation for change? Do you have any in mind, or perhaps you have tried to think out a few possible moves that will encourage collaboration in the most productive fashion? It could be in:

- **Understanding Your Coworkers:** It's you going beyond surface-level interactions by diving deep into understanding the backgrounds, experiences, and unique perspectives of your colleagues. Invest time in developing genuine connections on a personal level, even knowing a little bit about their life outside the office and how it might be influencing their attitude to their work or opinion on certain issues. By taking this initiative, you'll find yourself better equipped to truly appreciate the rich tapestry of diversity within your team and organization.

- **Uncovering Learning Goals:** Your role as a mentor or leader goes beyond giving guidance; it's about actively engaging with your mentees or team members. Spur them into conversations and sessions where they can speak freely, as it will give you the chance to take the time to explore what they aspire to learn and the skills they're eager to share. This approach is transformative, leading interactions into a two-way knowledge exchange where everyone contributes to personal and professional growth. In fact, the mentor and the mentee might find they both admire something unique about each other's approach, personality, or culture and want to know more or less about their different ways of doing things.

- **Promoting Leadership and Inspiration:** Encouraging your colleagues to step into leadership roles and inspire others is one of the many ways to promote DEI as a growth tool. It creates an environment where team members can lead and acknowledge the incredible value of each other's unique perspectives. This is the gateway to allowing innovations and fresh ideas to thrive and also nurturing a sense of empowerment among your peers. This brings to mind Sheryl Sandberg at Facebook, who champions women's leadership in tech. She inspired countless others to step up, get into training, explore their capacity to learn tech, as technical as it might seem, and then lead. Today, women make up 28% of the workforce in computer and mathematical occupations, and within the field of engineering and architecture occupations, women hold 15.9% of the available jobs (Women in Tech, 2023). Yes, the figures can be better, and it will be with more DEI initiatives to build upon, especially in the area of inclusion.

- **Building Strong Rapport:** One of the most rewarding foundations of a successful DEI strategy rests on meaningful relationships. Ensure you have these flowing interactions with your colleagues and team members where you can establish a level of trust and mutual respect through genuine connections. This is how an inclusive environment is nurtured, where everyone feels valued and heard. While Tim Cook, the CEO of Apple, is a simple man who values his privacy more than anything, he understands the importance of DEI and has cultivated strong relationships with both employees and customers, reinforcing the importance of genuine connections.

- **Prioritizing Minority Development:** In your capacity, make it a priority to advance the professional growth of underrepresented minorities within your organization. Remember, you are a role model, so ensure they receive equal opportunities and the necessary support for their development. A stellar example is Mellody Hobson, who has been a driving force behind diversity and inclusion efforts at Ariel Investments, working to elevate the representation of minorities in the financial sector.

- **Advocating Senior Leadership Buy-In:** Advocating for DEI initiatives and gaining buy-in from senior leadership is a critical part of every role model. You should convey the potential benefits and profound impact of these changes and show how great DEI can be for any workplace, especially yours when embraced at all levels of the organization. So many companies, knowing how helpful and insightful DEI has been since it was introduced, have had no choice but to create an agenda to stabilize its existence as it is a force that has come to workplaces to unveil a new culture of working in sync with each other.

- **Proactive Issue Identification:** Stay vigilant and proactively search for hidden challenges within your workplace, whether subtle or under-the-radar. Identifying these concealed issues allows you to address them early, preventing potential obstacles and cultivating a more inclusive and equitable environment. Much like how Google consistently seeks out invisible biases in its algorithms to ensure fairness and equality in its services. So, because they are up to speed in time, it cannot affect their productivity as they are able to nip it in the bud sooner rather than later.

- **Activate Activity Arcades:** With practical activities that will help connect role models with their coworkers, the journey toward DEI becomes easier. To engage in these activities is to forge individual relationships, build meaningful connections, and lay a proper foundation for collaborative efforts in advancing DEI and getting more familiar at the same time.

Activity Attempts

- **Three Statement Impact:** Most call this a "two-true and a-lie" game where coworkers form groups and exchange facts and fallacies about each other. Within the group, the game plan is to guess what is true and what is a lie in these statements. In doing so, it encourages team members to share personal anecdotes and colleagues to gain insight into each other's backgrounds and experiences for a deeper understanding of individual differences.

- **Find-A-Way:** This engaging exercise is all about survival and using each person's uniqueness to make headway for everyone. Here, team members discuss the items they would choose to have if stranded on a desert island. This conversation often reveals personal preferences and priorities, opening the door to understanding diverse viewpoints. If you know the game show "Survival," you will see that it's never easy to mingle or adjust to people who feel like strangers, but when DEI comes into play, there is no such thing as a stranger because it's all about inclusion and acceptance.

- **Nailed It:** Immerse yourself in a lively and inclusive Cultural Bingo game designed to deepen connections and celebrate diversity. Each participant receives a Bingo card filled with prompts related to cultural backgrounds, hobbies, and personal experiences. Here's the twist: your task is to do some friendly "snooping" to learn more about your fellow participants and fill in the Bingo squares accordingly. Engage in conversations, ask questions, and observe shared spaces to discover unique qualities. Once a row or column is complete, share your newfound knowledge with the group. This game goes beyond the ordinary, transforming diversity appreciation into a fun and meaningful experience that fosters a stronger sense of community. Let the cultural connections unfold, and enjoy the shared journey of discovery!

- **Quick Question:** Quick icebreaker questions, such as sharing the number of cups of coffee consumed in a day or favorite vacation destinations, is another way to lighten that overly busy and corporate atmosphere in the workplace with lighthearted conversations. It also gives room for personal preferences to be acknowledged and understood rather than misread like why a coworker always wears dark shades in the office. It could be because they have an eye issue or they are shy. Or, why does another coworker never use makeup? It could be for religious or personal reasons. All these are questions that can be answered when people get up close and personal.

- **Top Five:** This activity invites participants to share their top five favorites, whether it's movies, books, or travel destinations. So easy and fun and creates room for longer chats as people will be open to speaking more as to why they like this instead of that. It's a great way to explore common interests and spark conversations that transcend work-related topics.

Once you can activate any of these activities by introducing and playing along, count yourself ready and worthy as a role model.

You're already embodying the essence of a leader by actively engaging in DEI, regardless of your official title. Your efforts are instrumental in instigating change where it's needed. Now, you recognize that initiating change also means committing to modeling it and mentoring those around you. So, you're at the last piece of the puzzle going into the final chapter, which involves identifying pragmatic approaches to address challenges as the organization navigates this evolving landscape.

OVERCOMING DEI HUMPS

THE FINAL LAP

No culture can live if it attempts to be exclusive.
—Mahatma Gandhi (Teambuilding, 2022)

DEI and What Lies Ahead

As we navigate the intricate path of Diversity, Equity, and Inclusion (DEI) in the workplace, the challenges are endless. Workplace discrimination is an unfortunate reality that is deeply ingrained. To completely eliminate bias in today's world is a continuous effort because people still feel that sense of racial concerns as well as personal segregation. While DEI training is a cornerstone that helps ease these growing concerns, some of the most prevalent complications that hinder DEI initiatives must be faced and addressed.

In 2023, transgender workplace discrimination has come to the forefront, shining a light on the urgency of the issue with a 90% statistical figure showing it as the most prominent of all discriminatory behaviors (Fenton, 2023). It's a cause for concern, even though comprehensive data remains limited. For instance, looking into the story of

Laverne Cox, a notable transgender actress. Cox, known for her groundbreaking role in the hit series "Orange Is the New Black," faced discrimination and adversity on her journey to stardom. Despite the challenges she encountered, she emerged as a prominent advocate for transgender rights and an influential figure in the fight against discrimination. Her story emphasizes the need to tackle workplace discrimination head-on and find proactive solutions for the successful embrace of our DEI initiatives.

Dismantling workplace discrimination and promoting DEI is a multifaceted endeavor, one that demands recognition of the fact that significant transformation takes time and a ton of effort from role models and coworkers. It's imperative to understand that the DEI Lighthouse model emphasizes continually monitoring and adjusting your DEI plan. This phase of the journey is a linchpin in your pursuit of seeking a more inclusive workplace, requiring you to consistently assess your progress, anticipate potential obstacles, and ensure that your colleagues' needs align with the core values of your plan. Using the assessment framework elaborated upon in Chapter Two, you can systematically track progress every three months, showcasing your dedication to cultivating an environment where inclusivity thrives.

Also, in instances of entrenched workplace discrimination, where despite rigorous efforts, problems persist, it becomes essential to contemplate seeking legal counsel. Employment equity lawyers who specialize in addressing discrimination cases can be invaluable partners to your organization. They bring their expertise to the table, offering guidance on legal avenues and the necessary steps to rectify injustices. The pursuit of justice is a fundamental right, and these professionals can assist in ensuring that any discrimination is met with the appropriate response.

To mitigate the impact of workplace discrimination, understand common forms of discrimination and acquire the tools to respond effectively. Addressing these concerns proactively, before they escalate to the point of necessitating disciplinary actions, is paramount.

Getting acquainted with prevalent types of workplace discrimination, such as gender or racial bias, empowers you to take preventative measures and remediate issues when they arise. Recognize that the strategies expounded upon in your Chapter 3 plan prove indispensable in navigating these challenges. Not only do they equip you to tackle existing problems, but they also serve as a barrier to maintaining the effectiveness and integrity of your DEI initiatives so they remain robust and sustainable.

Complications

To give clarity to the actuality of DEI and discrimination, let's dive further into the likely issues in the workplace that spark the tension of discrimination:

Complication 1—Transgender Discrimination

Addressing transgender discrimination in the workplace is not just a matter of compliance but a vital mission, especially in a world where an alarming 90% of transgender employees have reported encountering harassment and inappropriate treatment within the past year (Fenton, 2023). To effectively combat transphobia (negative thought, action, or inaction towards transgender people) or to eradicate trans-prejudice, you need to deploy some practical strategies. One of the pillars of this effort is to ensure discretion and support for transgender colleagues experiencing discrimination. Giving them that safe haven so they can voice their concerns and ensure they are heard and revered is a key step.

In addition to promoting discretion and support, enact policy changes that bolster disciplinary actions in the face of discrimination. These changes send a crystal-clear message throughout the organization that discrimination, including transphobia, is unequivocally unwelcome and intolerable behavior. This, in turn, nurtures a workplace culture brimming with inclusivity.

Stepping into a leadership role, you mustn't underestimate the significance of providing practical and technical support to transgender employees. Recognizing their unique needs and offering a helping hand when necessary is a cornerstone of creating a supportive and appreciable atmosphere. Transphobia and unconscious bias training shouldn't be a one-time event but a continuous one. It will be a constant reminder of the organization's dedication to inclusivity and equip employees with the tools to challenge discriminatory attitudes and behaviors persistently.

Furthermore, to lower emotional disorders coming from transpeople's encounters with toxic workplaces, an extended warm welcome to them and non-binary colleagues is paramount. Start by dropping any expectations tied to pronoun usage and ensuring that everyone is well-versed in and respectful of their preferred pronouns. This harmonizes with an environment where individuals are free to express their gender identities without the looming specter of judgment or discrimination.

In the quest to eliminate the social stigma attached to gender diversity, consider the power of a sensitization initiative or a specialized workgroup. As a role model, try to run sensitization campaigns to educate your workforce about the unique challenges and experiences of transgender individuals, nurturing understanding and empathy.

Moreover, it's not just about words; actions speak loudly. Embed a robust anti-discriminatory policy within your organization, complete with unambiguous consequences for those who transgress. This sends a strong signal that discrimination in any form, including transphobia, is met with swift and proportionate repercussions.

Recognizing the significance of medical procedures for transgender employees is a cornerstone of support. It necessitates understanding and accommodating potential leaves required for medical appointments or procedures. Respect for employee privacy and choices in this domain is a must.

Respecting name changes is another vital strand of this tapestry. When a transgender employee decides to change their name, it's not just about making the switch but updating internal records, email addresses, and any professional order memberships. This administrative commitment symbolizes your respect for their identity.

Conducting anti-harassment meetings can be a turning point as well. By outlining explicit expectations for every employee, these meetings lay the foundation for an environment free from discrimination and harassment, where everyone is treated with dignity and respect. Let's not overlook the small gestures. Offering employees the option to indicate their preferred pronouns in emails and other communication channels is a subtle yet potent way to bolster support for transgender colleagues. This initiative contributes to a culture where sharing pronouns becomes a norm, fostering inclusivity.

Lastly, ensuring the availability of gender-neutral safety spaces or restrooms is not just about facility management; it's about ensuring safety and comfort. Transgender individuals frequently face violence and harassment in public restrooms that don't align with their gender identity. By providing gender-neutral facilities, you're not just facilitating inclusion; you're safeguarding the well-being and peace of mind of your transgender employees. This paves the way for them to navigate the workplace confidently and without the specter of discomfort.

Complication 2—Racial Discrimination

Tackling the pervasive problem of racial discrimination in the workplace is an ongoing quest for equality and justice. Shockingly, studies reveal that racial discrimination affects a significant portion of the workforce, with statistics ranging from 24% to 58% (Fenton, 2023). This goes beyond acknowledging the issue; it necessitates proactive involvement and transformative actions.

One potent strategy to combat racial discrimination is the formation and active participation in Employee Resource Groups (ERGs). As mentioned in an earlier chapter, these groups offer a platform for open dialogues and an exploration of diverse cultures, backgrounds, and experiences. It's a crucible for unity, where employees come together to share their distinctive perspectives and grow a workplace that embraces diversity with open arms.

In addition to ERGs, organizations must adopt a strict zero-tolerance approach to racism. Like transgender discrimination, this entails instilling comprehensive anti-racism policies, procedures, and clear-cut consequences for discriminatory behavior. This is not a mere bureaucratic task; it signifies embracing a set of core values that permeate every facet of the organizational culture. It's high time to shed light on and weed out any policies, behaviors, partnerships, or client relationships that run contrary to the commitment to eradicate racial discrimination.

A workplace free from discrimination necessitates a concerted effort to raise awareness. It's a collective responsibility to educate everyone about the richness of diverse cultures, the significance of different voices, and the persistence of injustices. The more informed and empathetic employees become, the more formidable the collective crusade against discrimination will be to make DEI thrive.

Respect and professionalism should be the bedrock of every workplace interaction. In leadership, awaken everyone's respect for cultural diversity, both in behavior and communication, and cultivate an environment where every individual feels valued and acknowledged. Furthermore, pledging to steer clear of racial slurs, offensive humor, or pranks is of paramount importance. When in doubt, it's best to leave such content outside the workplace. What may be a joke to you might be hurtful to someone else and cause an emotional breakdown. Watch your ways when it comes to statements, gestures, and dispositions.

Employees must proactively support anti-racism endeavors by promptly reporting any discriminatory conduct they encounter. Never keep silent but empower individuals to take a stand against injustice and reinforce the principles of equality and justice. Each report can be a significant step toward shaping a more equitable work environment.

In cases of racial discrimination complaints, it's imperative for organizations to treat them with gravity and handle them equitably. Every complaint should be subject to the correct procedures and resolved fairly and transparently. This ensures that justice prevails and sends a powerful message that discrimination is unwelcome.

The significance of maintaining an open-minded approach when addressing racial discrimination issues cannot be overstated. It is crucial to approach each situation with empathy, striving to grasp different viewpoints and lived experiences. This nurtures a culture of inclusivity and guarantees that every individual's voice is acknowledged and respected.

In instances where racial harassment adversely affects an individual's well-being and mental health, unwavering support is non-negotiable. The person experiencing discrimination should never feel isolated; their mental and emotional well-being must be a priority to avoid cases of depression and purported suicidal tendencies. The organization should stand alongside them in the battle against racial discrimination and all forms of aggressive behaviors.

Complication 3—Generational Discrimination

Now, a complex challenge affects a significant 45% of employees who demand proactive solutions that move beyond surface-level awareness (Fenton, 2023). An issue so threatening that as far back as 1967, the United States put forward an Age Discrimination in Employment Act to help successfully combat ageism. The idea is, why look at age if the ability, both mentally and physically, is still there to work and deliver? Also, why make people over 40 years of age feel like their life is over? Organizations must implement comprehensive strategies that bridge generational divides and foster an inclusive work environment.

An essential shift in addressing ageism revolves around recognizing and rewarding employee performance rather than tenure. By moving away from tenure-based rewards, organizations can cultivate an environment where employees are acknowledged and appreciated based on their accomplishments and contributions, ensuring that merit takes precedence over age-related biases. If Martin, a 55-60-year-old man, can still work well and hard at a factory as one of the attendants, then why should his position be sent over to someone young just because the organization believes Martin is unfit to keep working? It's a prejudiced way to judge efficiency and productivity in the workplace.

Hiring and promotion practices must be recalibrated to focus on skills, competencies, and potential, irrespective of age. Embracing a holistic evaluation of employees, free from age-based bias, creates a culture of meritocracy, where individuals from all generations have equal opportunities for growth and advancement. Tough decisions, such as layoffs, should never be driven by age-based considerations. It's crucial to avoid unfairly targeting older employees solely due to their age during challenging periods. Fair and unbiased evaluation, prioritizing skills and performance, ensures a just approach across generations.

Organizations can achieve a significant transformation by revising policies and wholeheartedly embracing a multi-generational workforce. This approach encourages teams with diverse age groups to collaborate and share their unique experiences and knowledge, recognizing the inherent value each generation brings to the organization's success.

Inclusive teams, projects, and team-building exercises provide a solid strategy to combat ageism. By promoting diversity within these contexts, organizations create a workplace where employees of all ages feel comfortable, valued, and empowered to collaborate effectively. Through these measures, organizations can cultivate a workplace that's free from generational discrimination, where every employee is appreciated for their unique contributions, regardless of their age. Remember Colonel Harland Sanders? It was in his early 60s he started Kentucky Fried Chicken (KFC). He began franchising his restaurant concept and the KFC brand in the early 1950s, and the first KFC franchise opened in 1952 when Sanders was around 62 years old. He went on to become a well-known and successful entrepreneur, helping to build KFC into one of the world's most famous fast-food chains. Now, everywhere in the world, KFC is the chicken delight for everyone. His skills had nothing to do with age but everything to do with efficiency, commitment, and ingenuity.

Complication 4—Gender Discrimination

Gender discrimination remains a persistent issue affecting a substantial 42% of employees (Fenton, 2023). Also, the findings, featured in the Academy of Management Journal and stemming from research conducted at the USC Marshall School of Business, highlight that workplace environments where gender discrimination exists can diminish the overall sense of belonging for both male and female employees (Gonzales, 2022). This complex problem includes disparities such as the gender pay gap and unequal promotion rates. To address this pressing concern, different strategies must be employed.

Transparency is the cornerstone of tackling gender discrimination. Companies must be forthright about matters like wages, job positions, promotions, and the reasoning behind promoting one employee over another. Openness can help eliminate gender biases by ensuring that employees are privy to the same information so they don't assume the worst.

Empowering women is essential to breaking through the glass ceiling by actively supporting them with the skills and potential to excel in senior positions. Another proactive approach that can help dismantle the barriers women often face and further implement gender-neutral recruitment processes through blind evaluation methods is a practical step to ensure candidates are assessed solely based on qualifications and skills rather than their gender. It promotes fairness and equality in hiring practices.

Also, conducting an equal pay review by identifying wage inequalities and standardizing salaries based on skills and qualifications rather than historical pay packages is a vital step toward wage equity.

Clear company policies and explicit consequences for harassment, discrimination, and inappropriate comments send a strong message that such behaviors will not be tolerated in the workplace. This promotes a culture of respect and inclusivity.

Recognize that gender discrimination extends to parental leave policies. Providing shared parental leave options can alleviate the discrimination men often face with paternity leave. Inclusivity in these policies encourages a more equal work environment.

Both men and women should have representation to ensure balanced and comprehensive policies in place. Inspiring and actively encouraging women to succeed without needing to justify their aspirations is a critical component of combating gender discrimination. This support and guidance can be a driving force for women to reach their full potential tirelessly and without any low self-esteem.

Promoting a culture of meritocracy, where skills and performance are prioritized over gender, helps recognize and reward deserving individuals. With this, everyone is given an opportunity to succeed. The fight against gender discrimination also demands that organizations offer equal opportunities for brainstorming, professional growth, and participation, creating a level playing field for everyone.

Lastly, it's essential to combat sexism and harassment with a robust anti-sexism and sexual harassment policy. This zero-tolerance stance against gender-based harassment, stereotypes, and discriminatory behavior reinforces a culture of respect and inclusivity.

Incorporating these strategies can help organizations address gender discrimination comprehensively so the workplace becomes a place where every employee feels at home and a part of something meaningful, irrespective of their gender.

Complication 5—Sexual Orientation Discrimination

Sexual orientation discrimination, which affects approximately 33% of employees, has grown over the years to become a bane in most working environments (Fenton, 2023). This statistic is not just a number; it represents the experiences of real people facing discrimination based on their sexual orientation. By acknowledging this fact, we take the first step in creating a workplace that values DEI.

Addressing orientation discrimination involves more than just awareness; it requires action. While introducing pronouns is a valuable step, it is equally important to implement concrete policies, conduct comprehensive training, and establish clear consequences for discriminatory behavior. These actions send a strong message that discrimination is not tolerated in the workplace and should not be kept silent. Beyond policies and training, offering resources and leave options for adoption or same-sex marriages is a tangible way to show support for LGBTQ+ employees. This not only recognizes their unique needs but also demonstrates the organization's commitment to equality.

Health insurance for same-sex partners is another move that can be made intentionally so employees, regardless of their relationship status, receive the same benefits. It reflects the organization's dedication to providing equal opportunities and privileges.

Supporting and welcoming transitioning employees to educate others can foster a deeper understanding of the challenges they face. This helps create an environment where everyone feels safe to be their authentic selves, and it promotes a culture of empathy and inclusivity.

Using appropriate terminology, particularly in job descriptions, is a simple yet effective way to support more gender-neutral language that not only respects all individuals but also sends a powerful message that the organization values diversity.

By incorporating these strategies, organizations can not only address sexual orientation discrimination but also lay the foundation for a workplace where every employee feels committed to work progress because their opinions and personalities are respected and regarded. This is the way to uphold legal and ethical standards and makes good business sense, as diverse and inclusive workplaces tend to be more innovative and successful.

So, empower yourself! Create a checklist using the one shown in Chapter 2 *(below)* that encompasses ideas for addressing the most prevalent workplace discrimination. Take the initiative to integrate the third column into your DEI pitch or plan, allowing for a comprehensive approach. Consider potential solutions for each discrimination type, mirroring the table example provided. Keep in mind that the final column is a dynamic aspect to be revisited every three months as you evaluate and measure the progress of your implemented changes. Draw inspiration from the sample to guide you through this transformative and impactful activity.

THE SITUATIONAL ASSESSMENT CHART

	1	2	3	4	5
	Current Situation	Data Supporting the Current Situation	Possible Complications Resulting From the Current Situation	Potential Resolutions/Ideas to Improve the Current Situation	New Data After 3 Months of Testing the Resolution
1	• Employees don't feel that the hiring process is fair.	• 9/18/23 employees listed the same issue.	• Poor employee retention and a lack of diversity.	• Change the hiring process to include equitable processes based on people's skills, and post new job listings on diverse job boards.	• 12/6/23 Employees believe the hiring process is more fair. • Alternatively, the sample data could show: 12/6 employees now list a new problem showing the lack of in-house promotions. • (This 3-month metric 73 reveals a new problem altogether)

EXAMPLE

So, knowing what you know now, can you say discrimination can be erased? Of course not, but understanding that its impact can be diminished is imperative. As the architect of your DEI plan, envision wielding a strategic tool to navigate workplace intricacies with finesse. You should always picture presenting not just an idea but a comprehensive blueprint meticulously designed to address and alleviate the subtle echoes of discrimination. This chapter encapsulates the essence of transformation, a poignant call to leadership, and a reminder that the power to reshape the workplace lies within your grasp. Begin with an idea, proceed with a plan, and get everyone on board regardless of character, personality, or orientation but focused on productivity. You will see that there is more strength in diversity than numbers.

YOUR FEEDBACK IS VALUABLE!

Hey there fellow leaders and readers,

I hope you've been enjoying this incredible resource. But here's the thing - your experience can be even more fulfilling, and it all starts with a simple question: How can you help others on their leadership journey?

Leaving a review for this book isn't just about sharing your thoughts; it's an opportunity to deliver value to fellow leaders, managers, and HR professionals who are seeking guidance and inspiration. Your words can make a difference in someone else's experience.

1. Click the link or scan the QR code below to leave an honest review on Amazon.

2. Share your thoughts, insights, and how this bundle has impacted your leadership journey.

By leaving a review, you're not just helping us; you're paying it forward to other leaders who are on their path to success. Your words of wisdom can inspire and guide them, making their journey smoother and more fulfilling.

So, let's come together as a community of leaders, share our experiences, and help each other thrive. Leave your review today and be a part of this incredible journey!

With warm regards,

Marguerite

CONCLUSION

~

This comprehensive journey through the intricacies of implementing Diversity, Equity, and Inclusion (DEI) in the workplace has equipped you with the essential knowledge and strategies. From understanding the core concepts to analyzing the need for specific interventions, you've delved into the intricacies of transforming workplace culture. Armed with data-driven insights, you've witnessed the power of introducing DEI concepts to organizational culture and policies, realizing that change can emanate from any level within the hierarchy.

As we move forward, the focus sharpens on fostering a curious mindset and breaking through biases via strategic training initiatives. Your role as a change agent is highlighted, emphasizing that innovation and transformation start with you. The exploration of practical ideas and exercises brings diversity into the workplace, stressing the importance of baby steps and collective efforts. No leader or executive should ever work with the assumption that they can do it alone. They need a team and a multifaceted one where you find all kinds of characters and personalities participating, and like a meal cooking, the end product becomes sumptuous.

Equity becomes a guiding principle delicately woven into the fabric of your organizational practices. This chapter underscores that DEI isn't just an acronym; it's a commitment to creating an environment where everyone has equal opportunities and feels valued. The final strategy encapsulates the culmination of your efforts, offering practical advice and exercises to enrich your workplace with inclusivity.

As you navigate the path to change, these chapters will place a mirror before you. It reinforces the truth that to advocate for transformation, you must embody it. The concluding message is clear: you are the epicenter of change. By incorporating the insights gleaned from these pages, you're not merely reading about DEI; you're actively shaping a workplace where diversity thrives, equity prevails, and inclusion becomes the norm.

In this final act, the spotlight is on you. Addressing the pervasive issue of workplace discrimination, this chapter acknowledges the difficulties in eradicating biases but provides a nuanced perspective. It recognizes training as a crucial tool and shifts the focus to addressing common complications in DEI workplace changes. Armed with the collective wisdom accumulated throughout this journey, you are poised to make a profound impact. The narrative concludes not just as a chapter but as a call to action, a powerful testament to your ability to drive change and champion inclusivity in a world that needs it. The journey has just begun; now, go and make a difference.

Embarking on the journey toward success was no overnight feat for me; it was a dedicated 20-year pursuit specifically tailored to benefit those facing discrimination in the workplace. My focus is now centered on crafting strategies that empower companies to leverage Diversity, Equity, and Inclusion (DEI) for the betterment of all, employing data-driven insights as the compass for change.

As we conclude this chapter, I invite you to become an integral part of the conversation. Your experiences, insights, and innovative approaches to measuring or implementing DEI strategies are invaluable. Let's break free from conventional boundaries and explore new perspectives collectively, harnessing the brilliance of previously overlooked creatives.

Your stories matter, and I'd love to hear them. Share your journey, your challenges, and your triumphs with me. Your voice adds a unique dimension to the ongoing narrative of creating inclusive workplaces. Don't hesitate to leave a review on Amazon, contributing to a communal pool of knowledge that can guide others on their DEI journey.

For those navigating the challenges of a demanding industry or company, I recommend exploring the book *Fearless Female Leadership*. It's a valuable resource tailored for women facing unique hurdles, providing insights and inspiration to navigate the professional landscape with resilience and courage.

As you continue your hard work and creative pursuits, I extend my heartfelt wishes for success and fulfillment. Your commitment to fostering change within your sphere of influence is commendable, and I believe that collectively, we can shape workplaces that embrace diversity, champion equity, and thrive on the principles of inclusion. Here's to your journey and the transformative impact you're poised to make. Cheers to the best and everything you truly deserve.

ABOUT THE AUTHOR

Marguerite Allolding, originally from a picturesque New England town, boasts over two decades of unparalleled leadership in the professional realm. Residing in New Jersey with her loving family, Marguerite's journey spans from the humble beginnings of her hometown, through the corporate corridors of Chicago, to the dynamic streets of New York. Along the way, she's secured influential leadership roles, consistently shattering expectations and challenging the status quo.

Marguerite's keen observations in the corporate world spotlighted the often underutilized talent of many women. These observations, combined with her personal experiences, fueled her to pen her debut work, "Fearless Female Leadership." Here, she celebrated the unique prowess of women in leadership, weaving intricate research with poignant narratives.

With this book, "Impactful Inclusive Leadership," Marguerite broadens her scope. While continuing to champion women's potential, she dives into the essential tenets of Diversity, Equity, and Inclusion (DEI). Through this new work, she crafts a compelling call to action, urging leaders of all stripes to cultivate truly inclusive environments where diversity isn't just acknowledged but celebrated.

Driven by an unwavering mission, Marguerite stands not only as a vanguard of change but as a testament to the transformative power of leadership that is both fearless and inclusive. She continues to inspire, guiding us towards a world that recognizes the strength in diversity and thrives on the pillars of equity and inclusion.

Also by Marguerite Allolding

Click link or scan QR code below to find Fearless Female Leadership: 9 Essential Strategies to overcome Gender Biases, Build Confidence and Empower Your career.

Also by Marguerite Allolding

Click link or scan QR code below to find Leadership Skills Unleashed: 18 Transformative Strategies for Managers at Any Level – Develop a Growth Mindset, Overcome Imposter Syndrome, and Create a Culture of Belonging

REFERENCES

SOURCE REFERENCES:

Affirmity. (2022, October 21). Employee Resource Group platform. https://www.affirmity.com/software/employee-resource-group-platform/

Analysis quotes. (n.d.). BrainyQuote. https://www.brainyquote.com/topics/analysis-quotes

Aspirale. (2023, May 4). *What is unconscious bias training for employees and why it's essential | Clear Law Institute.* Clear Law Institute. https://clearlawinstitute.com/blog/2021/06/07/why-unconscious-bias-training-for-employees-is-essential/

Barney, N., & Rosencrance, L. (2023). *diversity, equity and inclusion* (DEI). HR Software. https://www.techtarget.com/searchhrsoftware/definition/diversity-equity-and-inclusion-DEI

Benefits of Diversity in the workplace: What youth and Parents should know. (n.d.). https://www.bgca.org/news-stories/2022/December/benefits-of-diversity-in-the-workplace-what-youth-and-parents-should-know?gad=1&gclid=CjwKCAjwv8qk-BhAnEiwAkY-ahoEBqCjblmm5PWro8K3d1456Fhg_6R3-I8UQUZpolakeNHrd-BYmswhoCNbgQAvD_BwE

Best practices and tips for employees. (n.d.). US EEOC. https://www.eeoc.gov/initiatives/e-race/best-practices-and-tips-employees

British Heart Foundation. (n.d.). *10 Tips for Active Listening.* https://www.bhf.org.uk/

Bunch, H. (2022). *8 Tips: How to increase your knowledge on Diversity and Inclusivity — School store vending machine.* School Store Vending Machine. https://www.spiritboxnation.com/news/2020/6/10/8-tips-how-to-increase-your-knowledge-on-diversity-and-inclusivity

Council, F. C. (2020, March 24). *Mentoring For The First Time? 14 Tips To Start Off On The Right Foot.* Forbes. https://www.forbes.com/sites/forbescoachescouncil/2020/03/24/mentoring-for-the-first-time-14-tips-to-start-off-on-the-right-foot/?sh=799a977821a1

Diversity, equity, and inclusion plan template and tool | Office of Diversity, Equity and Inclusion. (2023, April 3). City of Philadelphia. https://www.phila.gov/documents/diversity-equity-and-inclusion-plan-template-and-tool/

Dunn, L. (n.d.). *What is Diversity, Equity & Inclusion (DEI)?* https://www.inclusionhub.com/articles/what-is-dei

Ellingrud, K., Ellsworth, D., Madner, S., Musallam, R., Sandhu, I., & Yee, L. (2023, January 13). *Diversity, Equity and Inclusion Lighthouses 2023.* McKinsey & Company. https://www.mckinsey.com/featured-insights/diversity-and-inclusion/diversity-equity-and-inclusion-lighthouses-2023

Employment Equity Training - The Mindspa Institute. (2023, July 10). The Mindspa Institute. https://themindspa.co.za/employment-equity-training/

Equity in the Workplace: What It Is and 9 Ways to Lead By Example. (n.d.). https://www.-betterup.com/blog/equity-in-the-workplace

Esparza, A. (2023). 12 Diversity, Equity, & Inclusion Activities To Kickstart Your 2023 DEI Initiatives. SnackNation. https://snacknation.com/blog/diversity-inclusion-activities/

EVERFI. (2023, August 24). *How to avoid age discrimination in the workplace.* https://everfi.com/blog/workplace-training/how-to-avoid-age-discrimination-in-the-workplace/

Fenton, M. K. (2023, June 8). Employment Discrimination Statistics In 2023. *Wenzel Fenton Cabassa, P.A.* https://www.wenzelfenton.com/blog/2022/07/18/employment-discrimination-statistics-employees-need-to-know/

Firstup. (2021). *15 ways to improve diversity and inclusion in the workplace.* Firstup. https://firstup.io/blog/15-ways-to-improve-diversity-and-inclusion-in-the-workplace/

Gino, F. (2021, August 30). *Unconscious bias training that works.* Harvard Business Review. https://hbr.org/2021/09/unconscious-bias-training-that-works

Green, R. S. (n.d.). *5 Ways to support Transgender and Gender Non-Conforming People in the workplace.* Great Place to Work®. https://www.greatplacetowork.com/re-sources/blog/5-ways-to-support-transgender-and-gender-non-conforming-people-in-the-workplace#:~:text=2.%20Display%20pronouns,can%20create%20tension

Hall, S. H. (2023, April 21). *9 Ways to measure the success of your DEI Strategy in 2023 - Senior executive.* Senior Executive. https://seniorexecutive.com/9-ways-to-measure-the-success-of-your-dei-strategy/

He, G. (2022, November 30). *70 Powerful Diversity And Inclusion Quotes For The Workplace.* teambuilding.com. https://teambuilding.com/blog/diversity-and-inclusion-quotes

Heinz, K. (2023). *What does Diversity, Equity and Inclusion (DEI) mean in the workplace?* Built In. https://builtin.com/diversity-inclusion/what-does-dei-mean-in-the-workplace

Hodgson, N. (2022, November 10). *Tackling transphobia in the workplace.* Raconteur. https://www.raconteur.net/talent-culture/transgender-discrimination-workplace

How to Define Company Values (And Why It Matters) | By Gustavo Razzetti. (n.d.). https://www.fearlessculture.design/blog-posts/how-to-define-company-values-and-why-it-matters

How to prevent sexual orientation Discrimination. (n.d.). Croner-i. https://app.croneri.-co.uk/topics/discrimination-and-equality/sexual-orientation-discrimination/how-prevent-sexual-orientation

Indeed Editorial Team. (2023, April 6). *13 Ways to Inspire and Motivate People in the workplace*. Indeed.com. https://www.indeed.com/career-advice/career-development/ways-to-inspire-people

James. (2022, March 8). What is Employment Equity? | Teamsters 987. Teamsters Alberta | Edmonton and Calgary. https://teamsters987.com/what-is-employment-equity-and-is-it-discrimination/

John F. Kennedy Quote. (n.d.). A-Z Quotes. https://www.azquotes.com/quote/547771?ref=equal-opportunity

Kohler, C. (2021). *What is unconscious bias training and does it work?* TopResume. https://www.topresume.com/career-advice/workplace-unconscious-bias-training

Kurter, H. L. (2020, July 22). *4 Ways To Create A More Diverse Workplace That Inspires Innovation*. Forbes. https://www.forbes.com/sites/heidilynnekurter/2020/07/22/4-ways-to-create-a-more-diverse-workplace-that-inspires-innovation/?sh=32c7793634af

Kurter, H. L. (2020, June 9). 4 Ways You Can Tackle Racial Discrimination In Your Workplace. *Forbes*. https://www.forbes.com/sites/heidilynnekurter/2020/06/09/4-ways-you-can-tackle-racial-discrimination-in-your-workplace/?sh=6be27fd60409

LAURIER, J. (2017, October 5). *Preventing and ending discrimination and harassment of transgender employee*. The Globe and Mail. Retrieved November 11, 2023, from https://www.theglobeandmail.com/report-on-business/careers/leadership-lab/preventing-and-ending-discrimination-and-harassment-of-transgender-employees/article36456796/#:~:text=It%20is%20also,of%20these%20leaves

Leadership Role Models | Qualities & Examples - Video & lesson transcript | Study.com. (n.d.). study.com. https://study.com/learn/lesson/role-model-leadership-style-examples.html

Leikvoll, V. (2023). Scale Up to 70% by Beating These 22 Unconscious Biases. Leaders.com. https://leaders.com/articles/business/unconscious-biases/

Leyshon, J. (2023, February 7). *10 ways to eliminate gender bias in the workplace*. Sage Advice United Kingdom. https://www.sage.com/en-gb/blog/eliminate-gender-diversity-workforce/

Making and handling complaints - Race discrimination - Acas. (2023, August 21). Acas. https://www.acas.org.uk/race-discrimination/making-and-handling-race-discrimination-complaints

Malyk, M. (2022). *What is Inclusion Training? Importance, Types, and Methods*. www.easyllama.com. https://www.easyllama.com/blog/what-is-inclusion-training/

Murray, R. (2023, March 8). The difference between DEI, CSR, and ESG - She+ geeks out. She+ Geeks Out. https://www.shegeeksout.com/blog/the-difference-between-dei-csr-and-esg/

Nguyen, D. (n.d.). Software Platform For Employee Resource Groups | Chezie. https://www.chezie.co/

Officevibe. (2023, July 17). *5 diversity and inclusion activities for the workplace*. Officevibe. https://officevibe.com/blog/diversity-and-inclusion-activities

OHCHR. (n.d.). *The struggle of trans and gender-diverse persons*. https://www.ohchr.org/en/special-procedures/ie-sexual-orientation-and-gender-identity/struggle-trans-and-gender-diverse-persons

Online Employment Equity – Copperline training. (n.d.). https://copperline.-co.za/corporate-training-courses/online-employment-equity/

Online, R. T. (2021, December 7). *Six traits of an effective role model for all managers.* Ready Training Online. https://readytrainingonline.com/articles/effective-role-model-traits/

Partners, F. (2023). *5 Tips: How to create a more Diverse Workplace.* Frederickson Partners. https://www.fredericksonpartners.com/news/blog/5-tips-how-to-create-a-more-diverse-workplace/

Pathak, A. (2023, April 27). *9 Powerful Steps To Eradicate Gender Inequality In The Workplace.* Nurture an Engaged and Satisfied Workforce | Vantage Circle HR Blog. https://blog.vantagecircle.com/gender-inequality-in-the-workplace/

Pathak, A. (2023). 26 Diversity and Inclusion Questions For Employee Surveys. Nurture an Engaged and Satisfied Workforce | Vantage Circle HR Blog. https://blog.vantagecircle.com/diversity-and-inclusion-questions/

Pathak, A. (2023). 6 Types Of Diversity Training For An Inclusive Workplace. Nurture an Engaged and Satisfied Workforce | Vantage Circle HR Blog. https://blog.vantagecircle.com/types-of-diversity-training/

Pathak, A. (2023). *7 Effective Ways To Promote Workplace Equity! Nurture an Engaged and Satisfied Workforce* | Vantage Circle HR Blog. https://blog.vantagecircle.com/workplace-equity/

Patterson, D. (2023, May 3). *3.5 Employment standards and employment equity.* Pressbooks. https://ecampusontario.pressbooks.pub/humanresourcesmgmt/chapter/3-5-employment-equity/

Peterson, M. (2023, January 11). 11 essential traits of an inclusive workplace. Limeade. https://www.limeade.com/resources/blog/inclusive-workplace/

Powerful diversity workplace statistics to know for 2023 | InStride. (n.d.). https://www.instride.com/insights/workplace-diversity-and-inclusion-statistics/

Qooper | ERG Software. (n.d.). https://www.qooper.io/erg-software

Reiners, B. (2023). *50 Diversity in the workplace Statistics to know.* Built In. https://builtin.com/diversity-inclusion/diversity-in-the-workplace-statistics

Sankofa, C. (2023, October 5). *Lead by Example Quotes To Talk About It And Be About It.* Everyday Power. https://everydaypower.com/lead-by-example-quotes/

Say, J. (2021, February 2). *Top 50 Inspirational Vision Quotes (SUCCESS).* Gracious Quotes. https://graciousquotes.com/vision/

Shi, D. (2022). *How to get better at using inclusive language in the workplace.* Fast Company. https://www.fastcompany.com/90753901/how-to-get-better-at-using-inclusive-language-in-the-workplace

Singh, D. (n.d.). *Your DEI-Centered Business Plan.* https://www.deannasingh.-com/blog/dei-business-plan

Staff, I. (2023, July 12). *6 top tips for preventing ageism in the workplace - Insperity*. Insperity. https://www.insperity.com/blog/preventing-age-discrimination/

Staff, L. E. (2023, August 22). *15 Tips for Effective Communication in Leadership*. CCL. https://www.ccl.org/articles/leading-effectively-articles/communication-1-idea-3-facts-5-tips/

Stainforth, D., & Null. (2023). A PRACTICAL GUIDE TO EMPLOYMENT EQUITY. Measuredability. https://measuredability.com/employment-equity/

Team, E. (2022, August 16). *Ageism in the Workplace and 7 Ways to Fight it | Embroker*. Embroker. https://www.embroker.com/blog/ageism-in-the-workplace-and-how-to-fight-it/

TestGorilla. (2023). *An HR professional's guide to DEI initiatives*. TestGorilla. https://rebrand.ly/a8sci5v

The Pyramid Principle - How to Effectively Pitch projects | Planio. (n.d.). Planio. https://plan.io/blog/pyramid-principle-pitching/

The Williams Institute at UCLA School of Law. (2023, February 14). *LGBT people's experiences of workplace Discrimination and Harassment - Williams Institute*. Williams Institute. https://williamsinstitute.law.ucla.edu/publications/lgbt-workplace-discrimination/

Tmason. (2022, April 11). *27 Fun getting to know you activities for work teams*. Outback Team Building & Training. https://www.outbackteambuilding.com/blog/getting-to-know-you-activities/

West, W. (2023). *10 Actions You Can Take Today to Be More Inclusive At Work*. The Diversity Movement. https://thediversitymovement.com/10-actions-you-can-take-today-to-be-more-inclusive-at-work/

What is diversity, equity, and inclusion? (2022). McKinsey & Company. https://www.mckinsey.com/featured-insights/mckinsey-explainers/what-is-diversity-equity-and-inclusion

Wong, L. (2023, March 30). Employee Engagement Surveys: Everything you need to know | Poll Everywhere blog. *Poll Everywhere*. https://blog.polleverywhere.com/employee-engagement-survey

Wong, L. (2023, March 30). Employee Engagement Surveys: Everything you need to know | Poll Everywhere blog. *Poll Everywhere*. https://blog.polleverywhere.com/employee-engagement-survey

WorkTango. (2023, August 9). *15 tips for building a more inclusive workplace | WorkTango*. https://www.worktango.com/resources/articles/how-to-build-an-inclusive-workplace

Yankovsky, D. (2023). *8 Tips To Boost Workplace Diversity In 2023*. Connecteam. https://connecteam.com/further-workplace-diversity-tips/

5 Ways to Assess a Company for DEI Before you Apply. (n.d.). https://resources.scrumalliance.org/Article/5-ways-assess-company-dei-apply

7 ways to be an inclusive co-worker – Inclusive Employers. (n.d.). https://www.inclusiveemployers.co.uk/blog/7-ways-to-be-an-inclusive-co-worker/

8 Great Job Boards for Diverse Professionals – AAUW: Empowering Women Since 1881. (2020, September 2). AAUW: Empowering Women Since 1881. https://www.aauw.org/resources/career/boost-your-career/8-great-job-boards-for-diverse-professionals/

10 ways to inspire others and change their life | Tony Robbins. (2021, December 31). tony-robbins.com. https://www.tonyrobbins.com/business/how-to-inspire-others/

11 Ways to Increase Workplace Diversity - ASME. (n.d.). https://www.asme.org/topics-resources/content/11-ways-to-increase-workplace-diversity

11 Ways to Increase Workplace Diversity - ASME. (n.d.). https://www.asme.org/topics-resources/content/11-ways-to-increase-workplace-diversity

25 effective diversity team building activities in 2022/2023. (n.d.). https://www.gomada.co/blog/diversity-team-building-activities

IMAGES REFERENCES:

** All images created by author**

Printed in Great Britain
by Amazon

49067772R00086